# THE ESSENTIAL GUIDE FOR THE NEW AGE OF RETIREMENT

## WHY THE RULES HAVE CHANGED

L David Overson

This document discusses general concepts for retirement planning and is not intended to provide tax or legal advice. Individuals are urged to consult with their tax and legal professionals regarding these issues.

Printed in the United States of America

First Printing, 2014

Gradient Positioning Systems, LLC
4105 Lexington Avenue North, Suite 110
Arden Hills, MN 55126 (877) 901-0894

# TABLE OF CONTENTS

# ACKNOWLEDGEMENTS

No man is an island. I'm grateful I wasn't alone in the authoring of this book. The words may be my own but the knowledge, concepts and ideas that grace these pages are attributed to many great minds, minds that have shaped my thinking and my life. Those sages are too numerous to mention here but their contributions, nonetheless, have been bronzed in my personal Hall of Fame.

I will acknowledge, however, the contributions of retirement specialist Bruce Smith for his out-of-the-box, brilliant analysis and ideas that have added to this work. I also want to thank Nick Stovall, CPA, for his valuable contribution to the tax chapters that follow. Many thanks, as well, to Anthony Wald and Ann Buffie for their editing and coordinating contributions. Kudos to the rest of the Gradient Positioning Systems team for their design and publishing contributions. And, of course, none of this would have transpired without the love, support, and patience of a wife who spent many an evening alone while I huddled in my man cave pounding the keys to fulfill this passion. Thank you, Kristy!

# INTRODUCTION

I'll never forget the day she came into my office. Even I was amazed by the story she told.

Mary was an attractive, fit woman in her early 70's with a kind, gentle demeanor that put me instantly at ease. It was our first meeting but it could have been our tenth. It didn't matter. We hit it off well. She had attended one of my financial workshops the prior week and felt the need to come in for financial advice.

As I began to ask questions about her situation, Mary revealed that her husband had died four months previous. She told me that they really didn't talk much about their finances. Bill liked to handle the money. She trusted him with it. He did his thing and she did her thing. It seemed to work well for them. But now he was gone and she didn't understand what her husband had done with their finances. She possessed little knowledge of investments and she was aware of it. What troubled her more was the fact that she was losing money every month. Lots of money. She was down about $400,000 in four months. The distress was clearly evident in her voice.

I began to peruse the brokerage statements Mary had placed in front of me. There were four, each from a different brokerage house. As I scanned the list of investments in each account, I was quite surprised at what I saw. Nearly every stock came from the technology field, names such as Oracle, Global Crossing, Palm, Solectron, Sun Microsystems and Compaq Computer. I could see that this was no average portfolio. A typical portfolio might contain a diversified mix of cash, bonds, large, high-quality stocks, some smaller, more aggressive stocks, and maybe even some international stocks. Not this one. I had never before seen such a high concentration of stocks in one sector of the market. Bill had plenty of money. He didn't need to take that kind of a risk.

It soon became apparent to me that Bill had rolled the dice with their investment accounts. This was a very aggressive portfolio. In all fairness to Bill, he had every right to be aggressive. It was his money. He had earned it. He could invest it any way he wanted. The problem was that Bill hadn't planned on two things that suddenly happened: his untimely death and the year 2000, the beginning of the end of the dot-com boom. That day, Bill wasn't sitting in front of me in the office – Mary was. And she was worried and seeking advice on how to correct the costly hemorrhaging of a net worth that was over $2.5 million the day Bill left the investment world for the spirit world.

This story has a happy ending, fortunately. Mary decided to transfer her accounts to my firm. I was then able to make needed adjustments in her portfolio that greatly reduced the risk and shored up the balance with a more reliable outcome. I was very happy with the final design. Mary was, too.

As the years have passed, I have met with Mary dozens of times for reviews and adjustments in her planning. She has since remarried. She's doing amazingly well in her late 80's. With each visit, the smile on her face has become, for me, a priceless validation of my efforts to make a positive difference in the financial lives of people.

Mistakes were clearly made in Mary and Bill's case, mistakes that could have been avoided by following sound principles of financial management. The following pages will address many of those principles. But there is a crucial fact that must be understood before we can proceed with any intelligent discussion of retirement planning or its principles. That fact is **change.**

**WARNING! Traditional retirement as you know it or as you've come to understand it is about to be turned on its head.** I will address in this book some of the reasons why I make such a brash statement and what you can do to prepare for the "new retirement" of the 21st century.

What has changed, you ask?

Gone are the days when you can earn a degree at an institution of higher learning, immediately find a job in your chosen career with full benefits, work your way up the company ladder over the next thirty-five years and then retire at age 65 with a pension, a gold watch, and a going away party stuffed with people you'll actually miss.

Gone are the days when you can contribute to a 401(k), IRA, or brokerage account with little knowledge or training in stock market behavior and average ten percent a year in return.

Gone are the days when you can save your money at fixed interest rates, outperform inflation, and earn enough interest to buy something more than a toaster and butter knife.

Gone are the days when government entitlement programs were healthy, funded adequately, and relied upon by all citizens as a blessing for hard work and effort instead of as a right.

Yes, a lot has changed. I will address in Chapter 1 a significant cause of many of the economic and financial changes we've experienced in this country over the last few years. And it's only the beginning of the changes that will occur. I am convinced that

America as we knew it and as we know it today will not be the same again, at least for decades to come. Because of these changes, many standard financial theories and concepts that worked in the past will not work well, if at all, in this new age of retirement. Every retiree and retiree wannabe will be affected by these changes. If you understand this changing environment, you can adapt. Otherwise, you will become an unwitting victim.

As for fundamental principles of retirement, the way you choose to approach retirement will impact your income, your taxes, your legacy and your emotional state of mind. It is a truism among financial professionals that when it comes to retirement *a few hours of planning can be worth more than an entire lifetime of working and saving.*

How is that possible? Because **retirement changes all the rules you have followed up to this point.** During your working years (the accumulation phase), you are able to take what I call "risk in the hope of greater gain." You don't need the money yet. It remains in your chosen investments. If you suffer losses, you have time to make them up.

Once you enter retirement (the distribution phase), you don't have a lot of time to make up losses if the risk doesn't pan out. In addition, you may need to withdraw an income to sustain your other income sources. You now can't afford to lose money since, as a result, your income payments may be reduced or a loved one may end up inheriting less of your hard earned assets. In other words, **the game has changed.**

The problem is that many retirees don't change anything about the way they invest or think about money. This is one of the many mistakes made in retirement planning: continuing to invest the same way after retirement that one invested before retirement. Why would someone do this? Because it's what they're comfortable with. It's what they know. It's always easier to follow what you know than to learn something new. Learning something new requires time and effort or money to buy better advice.

Retirement is more than kicking back and cashing in on your Social Security benefits. Not only are there thousands of different options for each individual that affect when and how to file for Social Security, there are thousands of options for how to invest individual retirement accounts (IRAs), 401(k)s and other investment portfolios. Investing is as unique as you are. Discovering the most efficient and effective way to invest your assets for a comfortable retirement requires professional advice and some elbow grease.

Think of it like this: You took time to choose your career, your educational path, your employment experience and your professional skill set. You chose a profession or a line of work that matched your skills and talents with your income needs. You probably spent some money getting educated or trained. Creating a retirement plan requires the same crafting and care that you put into your career. Your assets, your income needs, and your lifestyle are unique to you. They're different from anyone else. This is why **it is dangerous to seek financial advice from your friends and neighbors**. Did you ask them what career you should pursue, what church you should join, or which political party to embrace? If not, then why ask them how you should invest or plan the golden years of your life?

It's a sad fact that ***most people spend more time planning their vacations than they spend planning their retirement.*** The fact is most people do not have a good understanding of what they need to do for retirement. Not knowing what to do or how to plan for it makes it easy to default to procrastination. Putting off making decisions is a natural human reaction that usually hurts us or someone else. This choice can cause a myriad of problems that can greatly alter the course of your retirement.

This book is an attempt to share some of the vital principles that can help facilitate a more peaceful, rewarding experience in this new age of retirement. Whether you are anticipating retirement or already retired, this information can help you correct or avoid some of the common mistakes that can jeopardize your assets, your income, and your future way of life.

Let's begin with a discussion of why the rules have changed.

# 1

# THE MOST IMPORTANT NUMBER IN FINANCE

*If your outgo exceeds your income, then the upkeep will be your downfall.*

– Bill Earle

76 million! The most important number in finance in the 21st century. Yet most people are unaware of the impact this number possesses in the arithmetic of their financial future.

76 million! An astounding number that represents a select group of people in this country. This group of people is so powerful, so influential, so demanding, so numerous that when they sneeze, the nation groans at what might happen. These people have become indispensable to the American economy and our way of life. In fact, they helped create life as we know it in America today. They have infiltrated every element of society, from the boardrooms of business to the hallowed halls of Congress. No

element of American life in the last 50 years has escaped their fingerprint. This group's expected impact on our society and the world caused Time Magazine to vote this group "Man of the Year" in 1966.

I'm talking about the Boomers – babies born between 1946 and 1964. That eighteen year period following World War II produced the largest number of births in the nation's history. War has a tendency to bring us back to things that really matter. The nation – in fact the entire world – was hungry for healing and a return to normalcy after a bloody and costly contest. As life began to return to normal, the resulting spike in the birth rate added a wonderful new chapter to American history.

Boomers comprise 27 percent of the total US population, quite astounding when you realize there are only eighteen years between the oldest and the youngest in the group. The Boomers are clearly a force to be reckoned with, a massive placement of human capital in the economy. When they rock, the rest of America rolls. When they roll, America rocks. Yes, I'm one of them but I don't mean to pat my own back by patronizing the Boomers. I'm well aware of the fly in the soup. For now, let's focus on how the sheer size of the Boomer generation makes them the most important element in finance today.

## SPENDING AND THE ECONOMY

To begin, Boomers control over 80 percent of all financial assets in this country. It's no wonder. They created much of it through their innovation and desire to have more than their Depression-era parents enjoyed. They were a more privileged generation, conceived and raised by parents whom Tom Brokaw labeled "The Greatest Generation." Conditions were ripe at the time for these children to emerge in an improved economic environment that fostered their natural creative talents. Wonderful technologies and advancements occurred as this generation moved through society at large. The internet and its related accessories, cellular phones, lasers, medical resonance imaging (MRI), GPS, digital music, DNA fingerprinting, genetic sequencing, and yes, even Prozac, have all been invented or advanced during the Boomers' working years. As a result of these innovations, a record number of millionaires have been created during the last 40 years, a testament to the power of American freedom and capitalism.

The Boomers also comprise roughly one half of all spending in this country. They buy 77 percent of all prescription drugs and 61 percent of all over-the-counter-drugs. They account for 80 percent of all leisure/travel expenses. Why is all this important?

Spending is roughly 70 percent of the economy. An economy ebbs and flows according to the spending habits of its participants. For instance, when you buy a box of Lucky Charms (because they're magically delicious), you keep the store in business by moving product and earning a profit. The store then needs to replace the sold box of cereal with a new one therefore they order another box from General Mills, the company that makes them. General Mills keeps on making Lucky Charms as long as people buy them. Employees of General Mills get paid to make the cereal and send it to the store. They now have wages to spend. If more people buy the cereal, the company will have to hire more employees to meet the demand. More people are then put to work. Those people now earn a wage that will be used to buy, among other things, Lucky Charms for the breakfast table. More Lucky Charms sold means more profit for the officers of the company. They, in turn, buy breakfast at Starbucks because they don't have time for a Lucky breakfast. Starbucks then needs more lattes. This explains why Starbucks' stock has done so well. The process repeats itself. More people working means more dollars available in the economy to buy more Lucky Charms... and lattes. Everybody wins. The rising tide of increased spending lifts all boats. It's the circle of economic life.

Now let's trail the spending habits of the average citizen to learn how individual spending affects the economy.

As young people first enter the workforce, they begin to earn and spend. They contribute needed labor. The resulting paychecks get spent to buy goods and services. They move away from home and begin to build their own nest. They have babies. Now there is a need for more apartments, homes, furniture and diapers.

As these young people age and establish their careers, they usually earn more. The increased earnings result in increased spending on larger homes, better furnishings, newer cars and all the attendant trappings. By the time they reach their late-forties to early-fifties, they reach their peak spending years. The kids are now older, maybe even out of the house, and people start to reduce their spending. If there are any dollars left over at the end of the month, they direct them toward investments for retirement instead of a new home or a boat or Lucky Charms, thus reducing the amount available for spending on goods and services. When businesses sell fewer goods and services, they lay off employees, their profits decline and there is less spending in the economy. The spending tide goes out, lowering all boats.

Imagine what would happen if an immense generation of people began reducing their spending all within roughly an eighteen-year period of time? The first of the Boomers began retiring in 2011. This trend has already begun. The economy, the stock market, real estate and interest rates all will be affected by this immense change in the flow of money through the economy. Less spending translates into less profit for the companies that produce goods and services. Less profit means lower stock prices. Lower stock prices affect the value of retirement accounts. Lower retirement accounts create grumpy Boomers. No one likes a grumpy Boomer.

## THE DILEMMA

To complicate matters further, the Boomers made a few big mistakes as they chased the American dream. First, they forgot to have babies. Generation X, the children of the Boomers, number approximately 82 million. This averages out to 1.07 children per Boomer. We'll return to this issue in a moment.

Second, the Boomers continued the tradition of government-sponsored entitlements funded on a pay-as-you-go basis. The game has worked for decades but now the game is up. The government's own projections show the so-called "trust funds" that pay these benefits will start showing a deficit by as early as 2019.

Most people agree that the current system needs a reform. Congress has been debating the issue for years. The Boomers didn't cause the problem but they haven't solved it yet either. Attempts have been made to reform the entitlement process but in the end little has changed and the challenges still face us.

So what is at the heart of the issue?

If a company you work for wants to provide you with a future pension or other retirement benefit, they are required by law to fund that benefit in advance by making contributions to the plan. That's only logical. This assures that money will be there when the promised benefit comes due.

Government, however, is exempt from this law. Government doesn't have to pre-fund future benefits. The government pays current benefits out of the taxes collected from those who are still working. In years when more taxes are collected than are needed to pay benefits, the government spends them instead of investing the funds so they'll be there for future lean years. When those promised entitlements come due to the Boomers, their children will be stuck with paying the promised benefits. Simply put, robbing Peter to pay Paul has left Pat with the bill.

This brings me back to the baby issue. I mentioned previously that the Boomer generation produced 1.07 children per Boomer.

This is going to be a problem. A big problem. Here's the million dollar question: How will each child be able to pay enough taxes to pay for their own public services AND pay for Dad or Mom's retirement entitlements AND fund their own future retirement benefits AND pay the interest on a national debt created by the desire of those same parents and grandparents to maintain a certain standard of living at any cost? The answer is obvious - they can't. It is a problem of astounding magnitude.

## A PARADIGM SHIFT

This is the reason 76 million is the most important number in finance today. Like a cruise ship exiting a lock on the Panama Canal, just about everything will be affected by the movement of the Boomer generation into the next lock – the retirement years. Real estate, stocks, bonds and interest rates, the backbone of nearly every retirement plan, will react to this huge spending reduction wave, and those assets won't react the same way they have acted in the past. Stock market strategies that worked in the 1990s and 2000s will not work as well in the 2010s and 2020s, if at all. New strategies will be developed to capture a changing investment landscape. Investors who accept and prepare for this paradigm shift should weather it well with acceptable results.

In this complex and changing investment environment I believe there has never been a better time to utilize the advice of qualified financial professionals, especially those who specialize in retirement planning. Most investors simply do not have the time, the education nor the experience to navigate the retirement and investment waters that lie ahead of us. Too many, I'm afraid, will end up experiencing sub-par to poor results that will affect their peace of mind and way of life for years to come.

This wave of aging Boomers exiting the workforce and then consuming their investments throughout retirement will have the single greatest impact on retirement planning in the next 20 or more years. Everything will be affected by this wave. It is a predictable trend that has created a new age of retirement. If understood, this trend can help you plan better than you would otherwise. This book is designed to help you in that planning process.

## CHAPTER 1 RECAP //

- Boomers are 76 million strong and comprise 27% of the total US population.
- Spending is 70% of the economy.
- As aging Boomers change their spending habits into their retirement years, the economy will be affected in a major way.
- Understanding this demographic shift can help you plan better than you would otherwise.

# 2
# FUNDAMENTAL ELEMENTS OF FINANCIAL MANAGEMENT

*The pessimist complains about the wind; the optimist expects it to change; the realist adjusts the sails.*

         – William Arthur Ward

Will your Social Security benefits, savings and other retirement assets be enough? If you're like Jack and Beverly, you hope so. When the couple turned 60 years old, they started thinking about what their lives would be like in the next 10 years. When would they retire? What would their retirement look like? How much money would they need?

They could both count on Social Security benefits, but neither one really knew how much their monthly checks would be or when to file for them. Jack had a modest pension that he could begin collecting at age 67. He had always hoped to retire before that age. Beverly had a 401(k), but she wasn't exactly sure how it worked, how she could draw money from it or how much income it would provide once she retired.

While Jack and Beverly may sound like they're mostly in the dark about their retirement, the truth is that there are a lot of people just like them. They know retirement is coming and they know they have some assets to rely on, but they're not sure how it will all come together to provide them with a retirement income.

You spend your entire working life hoping what you put into your retirement accounts will help you live comfortably once you clock out of the workforce. The key word in that sentiment and the word that can make retirement feel like a looming problem instead of a rewarding life stage, is **hope**. You hope you'll have enough money.

Leaving your retirement up to chance is unadvisable by any standard, yet millions of people find themselves *hoping* instead of *planning* for a happy ending. With information, tools and professional guidance, creating a successful retirement plan can put you in control of your life.

While you may have built up a 401(k), an IRA, perhaps a pension and Social Security benefits, do you know what your financial picture is really going to look like?

Structuring assets to create an income-generating retirement requires a different approach than the one you used when accumulating and building those assets. Saving money for retirement, which is what you have spent your life doing, and *planning* your retirement are two different things. Both are important. Add the complexities of taxes, required minimum distributions (RMDs) from IRAs, and legacy planning and you can begin to see why happy endings require more than hope. They need a focused and well-executed plan.

There's obviously more to saving and planning for retirement than filing for your Social Security benefit and drawing income from your 401(k). The first step is to **create a strategy for your retirement** that can have a significant impact on those golden years. Understanding how to manage your assets entails risk management, risk diversification, tax planning and income planning preparation throughout your life stages. These strategies can help you leverage more from each one of the hard-earned dollars you set aside for your retirement.

Some people file for Social Security on day one of their retirement. Others defer the social security decision, relying on supplemental income from an IRA or other retirement accounts so their social security can grow. What is best? It depends on many factors.

## NEW IDEAS FOR RETIREMENT

Advice about what to do with money is as widely available as opinions on politics. Hindsight has always been 20/20. While there are some basic investment concepts that have stood the test of time, most strategies that work must adapt to changing conditions in the market, the economy and the world, as well as in your personal circumstances.

As I mentioned in Chapter 1, the Boomers have changed the retirement landscape for at least the next twenty years. The game has changed. The market downturn of 2008 highlighted how some investment strategies are not only ineffective but incredibly destructive to the retirement plans of millions of Americans. The dawn of an entirely restructured health care system in this country brings with it new challenges. These challenges will undoubtedly change the way insurance companies provide investment products and services. Add to the equation the unprecedented measures of the government injecting trillions of dollars into a struggling economy and you have even more unknowns to contend with in the future.

Perhaps the most important lessons investors learned from the Great Recession is that not understanding where your money is invested (and the inherent risks of those investments) can work against you. Saving and investing money is a great start but it isn't enough. Money must be managed prudently, which is a much bigger challenge for most people than saving it.

Essentially, managing your money and your investments is an ongoing process that requires customization and adaptation to a changing world. And make no mistake; the world is changing. What worked for your parents or even your grandparents, although appropriate at the time, will probably not work in this new age of retirement. Today, new ideas and professional guidance are the clarion call to retirees and pre-retirees.

Let's take a look at some basic elements of financial management as they relate to the new age of retirement.

## RIFT

I think we can all agree that the management of money is hardly an easy process. It takes time, knowledge and even some natural talent. In fact, for some people, money comes a lot easier to them than the ability to manage it wisely. **They just seem to have more dollars than sense.**

Just like any discipline, the ability to manage one's finances is a learned behavior. Like parenting, we get little to no quality instruction in the public school system on how to do it. Such learning usually comes as "on-the-job-training" which is a costly, trial-and-error experience that produces so many troubled children. This reminds me of a quote by P.J. O'Rourke: "Everybody knows how to raise children except the people who had them." So true.

When it comes to managing money, there are only four things you can control – the Risk you take, the Income you choose to take from it, the Fees you are paying and the Taxes you owe on the gains. I call this RIFT. Everything else about money is beyond your control and, therefore, not worth your worry and heartache.

By addressing RIFT in your portfolio, just about everything else takes care of itself.

Let's address each one individually:

**Risk.** You control how much risk you take with your money! It should never be left to someone else to determine. Risk is different for everyone. Some people possess a high tolerance for risk. Others do not. Age, investment experience, and goals and objectives all factor into the decision of how much risk a person should take.

The biggest mistake investors make, and they make it every day, is not understanding or wanting to understand the inherent risk of the investment choices they make. Because of this mistake, many investors take on far more risk than their own risk profiles would indicate is appropriate. They invest with "hope" instead of "information." Too many investors have the expectation that this time things will be different. "It won't happen to me" is a common belief among many investors. And on a regular basis, the markets of the world, whether it be stocks, bonds, real estate or commodities, remind us of the meaning of the word "risk." The ensuing losses provide costly experience that end up disrupting many well-laid investment plans. We will focus more on this topic later.

**Income.** Taking too much income or taking income from a fluctuating investment can wreak havoc on the best-laid retirement plan. For example, let's assume a portfolio of $100,000. Let's take 5 percent or $5,000 a year in income. That's $416.66 a month. If the portfolio consistently earned 5 percent interest or gain annually, you would still have the $100,000 a hundred years later. But it doesn't work that way, does it? Interest rates change. Stock prices change. Bond rates change. Everything changes.

So what happens when a portfolio earns less than the income you are taking from it? In the above example, let's assume the investment lost 5 percent one year. The $100,000 is now $95,000 and you received $5000 in income. This diminishes to $90,000 the following year. You've dipped into principal ($100,000 investment) in order to maintain your desired income level. Now the investment must earn over 11 percent the next year so you don't dip into principal again. If the investment loses 5 percent again the next year, you would need to earn over 24 percent ($90,000 - $5,000 income - $4,500 investment loss = $80,500 x 24.2 percent = $100,000) to return your principal to its original value of $100,000. And on it goes.

As you can see, this choice of income generation can be a ticking time bomb. Sooner or later it will explode. Take control of your income. Deciding to generate most or all of your income from guaranteed sources instead of risk-oriented sources is the wisest choice for a more predictable retirement.

**Fees.** Other factors that erode your return on investment are the costs and fees you pay for professional services. These fees include fund management fees, service fees, trading fees and advisor fees for managing your money. Don't get me wrong. As an advisor, I clearly see the merits of good professional money management. If the fund performs better than its peers, then the fees are well spent. If the financial advisor managing your account performs up to your expectations, then the fee is also money well spent.

Where a serious problem arises is when the performance does not merit the cost of the services provided. I remember analyzing a portfolio early in my career where a $200,000 brokerage account had grown only $50 over a three-year period of normal stock market performance. The broker had made so many trades in three years that all the gains earned had been eaten up by trading fees, commissions and losses on trades. This is an unusual example but the fact remains that some fees are just not worth it.

Take control of the fees you are paying, and make sure what you're getting is worth the fee.

**Taxes**. Another factor diminishing the success of your portfolio is taxes. Although I will address this topic in greater detail in a later chapter, suffice it to say that taxes are a bigger problem than the fees just discussed. They're much larger for one thing. But what do you really get for the taxes you pay on gains? At least with fees, you get something such as management, trading, etc. You get nothing for the taxes you pay on your investments. It's simply the price you pay for the choice of investments you make. Choose different investments and you'll pay less or no tax at all. I've always said that reducing your taxes is a right. Exercise it. Let your neighbors pay more tax. It's OK. This is America!

## "I HOPE SO" VS. "I KNOW SO" MONEY

There are essentially two types of money: *I Hope So* Money and *I Know So* Money. All your assets can be divided into these two general categories. You may have more of one kind than the other. The goal isn't to eliminate one type of money but to find a proper balance that suits your particular goals and objectives.

*I Hope So* Money is money that is at risk in the hope of greater gain. It fluctuates with the markets. It has no minimum guarantee. It is subject to investor activity, stock prices, market trends, buying trends, etc. You get the picture. This money is exposed to greater risk but also has the potential for greater reward. Because the market is subject to change, you can't really be sure what the value of these investments will be in the future. You can't really *rely* on these monies at all. For this reason we refer to it as *I Hope So* Money. This doesn't mean you shouldn't have some money invested **in the hope of greater gain**. But it is dangerous to assume that you can know what it will be worth in the future.

*I Hope So* Money is an important element of a retirement plan, especially in the early stages of planning when you can trade volatility for potential returns and when a longer investment time horizon is available to you. In the long run, time can smooth out the ups and downs of exposure to the inherent market risks of any risk-oriented investment.

*I Know So* Money, on the other hand, is the safer money in the portfolio. This money is made up of dependable, low-risk or guaranteed accounts. Social Security is one of the most common forms of *I Know So* Money. Income you draw or will draw from Social Security is guaranteed. You have paid into Social Security your entire career, and you can rely on that money during your retirement. Unlike the stock market, the rate of growth for many *I Know So* accounts is based on 10-year treasury rates. The 10-year treasury, or TNX, is commonly considered to represent a very secure and safe place for your money. The 10-year treasury drives key rates for things such as mortgage rates and CD rates. *I Know So* Money may not be as exciting as *I Hope So* Money, but it has a more predictable outcome and therefore is a valuable tool in planning one's retirement.

Over the years I have reviewed hundreds of portfolios for prospective clients seeking retirement planning advice. I can say without hesitation that the more *I Hope So* monies a client wants in the portfolio, the more difficult it is to provide that client with a predictable outcome. Why? Because making any kind of projection on assets that are at risk is nothing more than making a guess. Sure, you can study the past performance of an investment and hope it repeats itself but there is no assurance that it will. This is why every investment prospectus is required to contain the words, "past performance is not indicative of future performance," or words to that effect. You might as well make a bet on who will make it to the Super Bowl next year as project a certain monthly income payment from a risk-oriented portfolio over your lifetime.

There are just too many factors we can't control when it comes to *I Hope So* monies. It's unwise to leave the future of your retirement to a guess. The more *I Know So* monies you have in the portfolio, the less volatility or risk you have to contend with.

For example, in the early 1990s, interest rates were high and market volatility, or risk, was low. Back then, you could invest in either type of money and be rewarded with a reasonable risk-adjusted return. Since 2007, however, stock market risk has risen significantly. Volatility has been at all-time highs. Interest rates, however, have been at all-time lows, the opposite of the early 1990s. This scenario has forced more and more investors to take market risk in order to obtain a reasonable return on their money. The increased buying of stocks and bonds has driven up prices once again to all-time highs for some stock indices. Investors have been giddy with delight.

Investors, however, have forgotten one very important fact. The stock market didn't regain its losses from 2008 and 2009 until the summer of 2013. In other words, stocks went five years without earning a return for investors. That's hardly anything to be giddy about. Many retirement plan projections blew up. They weren't worth the paper they were written on. Many investors had to go back to the drawing board and make new guesses or projections in their planning. Some now suffer reduced monthly income payments from their portfolio. Either way, it has been an unfortunate result of risk doing what risk has always done: create uncertainty. Too much uncertainty is a dangerous planning tool to rely on during your golden years.

## HOW MUCH RISK ARE *YOU* EXPOSED TO?

Many investors really don't understand how much risk they are taking in their portfolios. It is helpful to organize your assets into categories so you can have a clear understanding of how much of your money is at risk and how much is in safer holdings.

Let's review the two types of money again:

**I Hope So** Money is, as the name indicates, money that you *hope* will be there when you need it. *I Hope So* Money represents what you would like to get out of your investments. Examples of *I Hope So* Money include:

- Stocks and bonds
- Mutual funds and ETFs
- Variable annuities
- REITS

**I Know So** Money is money that you know you can count on. It is safer money that isn't exposed to the level of volatility as the asset types noted above. You can more confidently count on having this money when you need it. Examples of *I Know So* Money are:

- US Government securities
- Savings and checking accounts
- CDs
- Fixed annuities

Determining the amount of risk that is right for you is dependent on a number of factors. You need to feel comfortable with where and how your money is invested. Working with a qualified financial professional makes this risk analysis easier. A financial professional is obligated to help you understand the risk of any investment you may be considering as well the suitability of that investment in your particular situation.

Managing your risk by having a proper balance of both types of money is a good place to start. The proper balance for you depends on your age, risk tolerance, income needs and how much safe money (i.e., social security, pensions, etc.) that you already have in your plan.

So, how do you begin to know how much risk you should be exposed to?

While there is no single approach to determining the appropriate risk you should take, there are some helpful guidelines. A good place to start is to use *The Rule of 100*.

## THE RULE OF 100

The average investor needs to accumulate assets to create income during retirement. To accomplish this, they need to balance the amount of risk to which they are exposed. Some risk is prudent since *I Know So* Money, being safer and more reliable, doesn't grow very fast, if at all. Today's historically low interest rates don't even keep up with inflation. *I Hope So* Money, while less dependable, has more potential for growth. This type of money can eventually be converted to safer money at an appropriate time when risk is no longer needed or wanted.

The Rule of 100 is a general rule that helps shape asset diversification for the average investor. The rule states that the number 100 minus your age equals the amount of assets you should have at risk. As you age, the Rule indicates that you should reduce the amount of your assets at risk by increasing the amount of safe monies in your portfolio.

For example, if you are a 30-year-old investor, the Rule of 100 indicates that you should focus on investing 70 percent of your assets in stocks, bonds, mutual funds and real estate. It would be prudent to invest the remaining 30 percent in CDs, cash, and fixed annuities.

Now, I'm not saying that every 30-year-old should have 70 percent of their assets in risk-oriented investments. The Rule of 100 is based on your chronological age, not your "financial age". Financial age is based on your understanding of investments, your investment experience, your aversion or acceptance of risk and other factors. While this rule isn't an ironclad solution to asset diversification, it's a good place to start. Once you've taken the time to look at your assets to determine your risk exposure, you can use the Rule of 100 to make changes that put you in a more stable investment position – one that reflects your comfort level, risk tolerance and your goals.

Perhaps when you were age 30 and starting your career, like in the example above, it made sense to have 70 percent of your money in the market. You had plenty of time to save more money, work more and recover from a downturn in the market. Retirement was ages away and your earning power was increasing. Younger investors should take on more risk for exactly these reasons. The potential reward of long-term involvement in the market outweighs the risk of investing when you are younger.

Risk tolerance generally reduces as you get older, however. If you are 40 years old and lose 30 percent of your portfolio in a market downturn this year, you have 20 to 30 years to recover the losses. If you are 68 years old, you have only a few years to make the same recovery. That new circumstance changes your whole retirement perspective. At age 68 it's likely that you simply aren't as interested in suffering through a tough stock market. There is less time to recover from downturns and the stakes are higher.

The money you have saved is money you will soon need in order to meet your income needs or to meet the income needs of a spouse or loved one.

The great advantage of investing earlier in life is related to *compounding*. Compounded earnings can be incredibly powerful over time. The longer your money has time to compound, the greater your wealth. This is what most people talk about when they refer to putting their money to work. This is also why the Rule of 100 favors risk for the young. If you start investing when you are young, you can invest smaller amounts of money in a more aggressive fashion because you have the potential to earn gains that then compound over time. When you are 50 or 60 years old, the compounding potential decreases. If you don't feel you have enough assets to retire on at these older ages, you feel the need to take on more risk, which can be a dangerous decision if the investments don't pan out.

Let's look at another example that illustrates how The Rule of 100 becomes more critical as you age. An 80-year-old investor who is retired and is relying on retirement assets for income, for example, needs to depend on a predictable amount of *I Know So Money*. The Rule of 100 says an 80-year-old investor should have a maximum of 20 percent of his or her assets at risk. Depending on the investor's financial position, even less risk exposure may be preferable. You are the only person who can make this kind of determination. Everyone has their own level of comfort. Your Rule of 100 results will be based on your values and attitudes as well as your risk tolerance.

The Rule of 100 can be used to allocate specific investment accounts, too. Take 401(k)s as an example. Many people have them, but not many people understand how their money is allocated within their 401(k). An employer may have provided someone who comes in once a year to explain the options in the plan but that's as much guidance as most 401(k) participants get from the plan. Following the Rule of 100 will give you a better mix of risk and safe monies in your plan. Many 401(k) options include target date funds that change their risk exposure over time, essentially following a form of the Rule of 100. Selecting one of these options can often be a good decision because the fund automatically reallocates risk for you as the stated target date approaches.

## OPTIMIZING RISK AND FINDING THE RIGHT BALANCE

The Rule of 100 is a useful tool to determine the appropriate risk you might want to take. Remember, it's just a baseline or starting point. The Rule of 100 would suggest a 50-year-old would hold 50 percent of their assets in Green Money and 50 percent Red Money. Most 50-year-olds are more risk tolerant, however. There are many reasons why someone might want to take on a little more risk. Investors who are experienced or who have already met their retirement income goals and are looking for additional ways to accumulate wealth are all candidates to consider more risk. Before you make the decision to assume more risk, ask yourself this question: How much can I afford to lose? By assuming you'll lose the additional monies you put at risk, you are in the most logical position to make a decision about risk.

Consider the following scenario: You have $100,000 saved that you would like to invest in the stock market. The portfolio you've chosen could turn your $100,000 into $120,000 by next year or it could lose $20,000, leaving you with $80,000. Is this a gamble you're willing to take? Your answer to this question will help determine the appropriate balance of risk and safety that is right for you.

When the rubber meets the road, the expected or historical return on any investment option will probably dictate your choice. If the expected return from an investment won't meet your retirement goals, you most likely will choose an investment that does, regardless of the risk. For example, if the historical return of a certain investment has averaged 6 percent and you've determined that you need an 8 percent return to meet certain retirement goals, you may be tempted to take more risk and chose an investment that gives you what you want. Your financial professional may even encourage you to be more aggressive with your investment strategy. Beware, however! If taking more risk isn't an option that you are comfortable with, then the discussion should turn to how you can earn more money with less risk or how you can spend less in order to align your needs with your risk tolerance. Taking more risk to satisfy present wants often jeopardizes your future wants. Will it be worth it? Only you can decide.

## CHAPTER 2 RECAP //

- Focus on the four things you can control in your planning: risk, income, fees, and taxes (RIFT).
- •Work on obtaining the proper balance of *I Know So* Money and *I Hope So* Money for your particular situation.
- Let the power of compound interest work for you. Start saving more now.
- •Use the Rule of 100 as a general guiding principle when determining how much risk you should take in your portfolio.

# 3
# THE COLOR OF MONEY

*Rule #1: Never lose money.*
*Rule #2: Never forget Rule #1*

— Warren Buffett

Going a step further, we can organize the types of investments and assets you have into a helpful visual schematic.

It can be helpful to assign colors to the different types of money and their level of risk. For our purposes, *I Know So* Money (which is safer and more dependable) we'll call **Green Money**. *I Hope So* Money (which is exposed to risk and fluctuates with the market) is **Red Money**. A third type of money - a blend of the first two types - is **Yellow Money.** This is money in which the risk is reduced because it is being professionally managed with a strategy.

A sad fact is that too many people don't know their level of exposure to risk. Whether you are a retiree or a pre-retiree, visually organizing your assets is an important and powerful way to get a clear picture of what kind of money you have, where it is and how you can best utilize it in the future. This process is as simple as listing your assets and assigning them a color based on their status. Comparing the color of your investments will give you an idea of how well you are following the Rule of 100 discussed previously. You will probably be surprised at how much Red Money you have in your portfolio.

Over the course of your lifetime, it is likely that you have acquired a variety of assets such as savings accounts, 401(k)s, IRAs, pensions and possibly real estate. You have earned money from your chosen career and have made financial decisions based on the best information you had at the time. When viewed as a whole, however, you might not have an efficient strategy for the management of those assets. As we have seen, it's more important than ever to know which assets are at risk. High market volatility and low treasury rates make for a challenging maze in which to plan retirement. Navigating this maze starts with knowing what kind of risk you are taking.

Even if you feel that you have plenty of money in your 401(k) or IRA, misunderstanding the risk you are taking can cause major financial suffering. Take the market crash of 2008 as an example. In 2008, the average investor lost over 30 percent of their 401(k), IRA or other stock market accounts. So did many real estate investors. If more people had shifted their investments away from risk as they neared retirement - if they had followed The Rule of 100 - they might have suffered less dramatic declines in account value and would be closer to meeting their retirement goals today.

Investing heavily in Red Money is incredibly risky no matter where you fall within the Rule of 100. Red Money cannot be depended on to generate stable income and a plan that leans too heavily on Red Money can easily fail, especially when investment decisions are influenced by emotional reactions to market ups and downs. Emotional investing is not only unwise, it can be very stressful during the time in your life when you expect to be stress-free.

Green Money is no cure-all for a retiree either. A plan that uses too much Green Money can also possess challenges. Investing too much money in Certificates of Deposits (CDs), savings accounts, money market accounts or other low-return accounts may not keep pace with inflation – the phantom tax. Without some growth in the portfolio (Red or Yellow Money), you have less chance of earning more than the rate of inflation over time and therefore staying ahead of it. The Rule of 100 can help you determine an appropriate mix of Red, Yellow and Green Money for a balance of safety and growth.

Green Money becomes more important as you age. As you reduce the amount of Red Money in favor of Green Money, it's important to separate the Green Money into two types: **Need Now** money and **Need Later** money.

## TYPES OF GREEN MONEY:

**Need Now** money is money used to meet your basic needs, including your bills and the costs associated with maintaining your lifestyle. It may also include other needs such as a planned vacation, ongoing health treatments not covered by insurance, needy children or parents or other immediate needs.

**Need Later** money is money that you don't need now for income or other immediate needs but will need sometime in the future. A reserve fund or emergency fund are both examples of Need Later money. I always recommend a healthy reserve fund for those unexpected expenses that seem to surprise us all from time to time. As a financial planner, I do not invest all the funds a client may have available. Some money needs to remain in the bank for a reserve. No, it may not earn much sitting in the bank but knowing that a client has liquidity allows me to commit other funds to better-performing financial vehicles. Maintaining a reserve fund just makes good sense, like looking both ways before crossing a street. Sooner or later you'll be glad you did.

## YELLOW MONEY

Now that you've calculated the Rule of 100 and have determined how much safety you ought or want to have in the portfolio, it's time to look at the Red Money.

According to a recent DALBAR report, the deck is stacked against the risk-oriented retiree. The report shows that the average investor on a fixed income failed to keep pace with inflation in nine of the last 14 years, meaning the inherent risk in managing your Red Money by yourself is very real and could have a lasting negative impact on your assets (see Chapter 8).

So, how exactly do you invest your Red Money? There are a myriad of options, including stocks, bonds, mutual funds, exchange-traded funds (ETFs), variable annuities, real estate, options, commodities and futures. There are a lot of different directions in which you can take your Red Money. One thing is for sure: growth potential depends on taking some risk. Choosing stocks, bonds and funds together in a portfolio without a cohesive strategy behind them could cause you a lower return and/or unneeded risk. The end result is that you may never really understand what your money is supposed to be doing. While you may have expectations for each individual asset in your portfolio, those assets may actually be working against each other without your knowledge.

Enter **Yellow Money.** Yellow Money is money that is managed by a professional *with a purpose*. After your income needs are met, whether you're retired or still working, you may have assets that you would like to dedicate to accumulation. Should they be invested as Red Money or Yellow Money? It depends.

The difference between Red Money and Yellow Money is that Yellow Money has a cohesive strategy behind it that is implemented by a professional. Yellow Money is money that is being managed with a specific purpose. Yellow Money is still a type of Red Money but it comes with different levels of risk. Yellow Money is under the watchful eye of professionals who have a stake in the success of your money. They can recommend a range of investment strategies to fit your particular risk tolerance.

It can be helpful to think of Red Money and Yellow Money with this analogy:

If you needed to travel through an unfamiliar city in a foreign country you could rent a car or hire a driver. Were you to drive yourself, you could follow the guidance of perplexing road signs as your stress and worry mount. It would probably take longer to get to where you want to go and the chance of a traffic accident would also increase. If you're male, it would take even longer because you wouldn't dare stop and ask for directions. But if you hired a driver, you could sit back and enjoy the ride with little worry about which is the fastest or safest course to get you there.

Red Money is like driving the car yourself. Yellow Money is like hiring a driver. You're still in the same car but now you have a professional working on your behalf who knows a faster, safer route to take. And men can avoid the embarrassment of stopping to ask for directions.

## TAKING A CLOSER LOOK AT YOUR PORTFOLIO

Think about your investment portfolio as it relates to your retirement goals. Is it really worth jeopardizing your future income or goals by trying to manage your Red Money by yourself? Harnessing the earning potential of your Red Money requires more than a collection of stocks, bonds, mutual funds, a wing and a prayer. It requires expertise. A good money manager uses this expertise to allocate assets in such a way as to control the risk while trying to generate the best possible returns in a given market condition. When the market changes, the money manager adjusts the allocation to maximize return or to preserve existing gains in the port-folio while staying within the stated risk tolerance of the investor. In short, the main reason to hire a professional money manager is **to reduce risk.** That reduced risk makes Yellow Money a more reliable tool for retirement planning than Red Money.

Some financial professionals have the expertise to manage money and some do not. Those that don't manage money them-selves usually offer this service through a third party money man-ager. Either way, anything worth having is worth paying for and money managers do charge a fee for their services. The fees can range anywhere from a quarter of one percent to over 2 percent, depending on the amount of money under management, the style of management and the performance history of the manager. As I mentioned previously, fees are worth it as long as you're getting something of value for it. Reducing risk is worth a fee, in my opinion.

## CASE STUDY

*Janet is 65 years old and wants to retire in two years. She has a 401(k) that she has contributed to for 26 years. She also has some stocks that her late husband managed. Janet also has $55,000 in a mutual fund that her sister recommended to her five years ago and $30,000 in another mutual fund that was recommended by a friend. Looking at her portfolio, Janet decides that she doesn't understand much about mutual funds, stocks or the risk she is taking. She decides to meet with an investment advisor who then asks the following questions:*

***1. Does she know exactly where all of her money is?*** *Janet doesn't know much about her husband's stocks, which she now owns. She knows the value is about $100,000 and they represent three well-known companies. Janet doesn't know anything about the financials of these companies and doesn't know if she should sell them or hold them.*

**2. Does she know what types of assets she owns?** *Yes and no. She knows she has a 401(k) and IRAs, but she is unfamiliar with the investment options in each or how they are individually performing. Furthermore, she is unclear as to how to manage the holdings as she nears retirement.*

**3. Does she know the strategies behind each one of the investment products she owns?** *While Janet knows she has a 401(k), an IRA, and mutual fund holdings, she doesn't know how to reallocate these accounts if the market were to tumble next week. She is unsure whether her IRA is a Roth or a traditional IRA and she is unsure how to draw income from it after retirement. Sadly, Janet does not have specific investment principles guiding her investment decisions. She is also concerned about how these assets will pass on to her children after death.*

*After analyzing Janet's assets, her advisor prepares a consolidated report that lays out all of her assets for her review. The advisor explains each one of them to her. Janet discovers that although she is two years away from retiring, her 401(k) is allocated with more risk than is appropriate for her age and objectives. She will need additional monthly income from the 401(k) to meet her needs. Since 65 percent of her 401(k) is at risk, she agrees to reduce the risk. She likes the Rule of 100 report which suggests placing only 35 percent at risk. She agrees to hire the advisor to manage the 401(k) to reduce risk and hopefully improve performance. The advisor also points out several instances of overlap in her mutual fund holdings. Janet learns that while she is comfortable with one of her mutual funds, she does not agree with the management principles of the other.*

In the end, Janet's advisor helps her reallocate her 401(k) from Red Money to Yellow Money. This reduces the risk and helps prepare the plan for income distribution in two years. Her advisor also uses her mutual fund and stocks to create a growth oriented investment plan that will help offset the impact of inflation. Since she plans on relocating closer to her children and grandchildren, these accounts will come in handy later in her life.

By creating an overall investment strategy, Janet is able to meet her targeted goals in retirement. In addition, the advisor will work closely with her tax professional to minimize the tax impact of any changes to her portfolio in the future.

You may have a better understanding of your assets than Janet did, but even someone with an investment strategy can benefit from having a financial professional review their portfolio.

## CASE STUDY

*Charles is 69 years old. He retired four years ago. He relied on income from an IRA for three years in order to increase his Social Security benefit. He also made significant investments in 36 different mutual funds. He chose to diversify among the funds by selecting a portion for growth, another for dividends, another that focused on promising small companies and the remainder for index funds. All the money that Charles had in mutual funds was earmarked as Need Later money. After the stock market took the hit in 2008, Charles lost confidence in his investments and decided to sit down with a financial advisor to see if his portfolio could recover.*

*The advisor was able to determine the goals and objectives Charles had for retirement. The advisor also analyzed each of the mutual funds and discovered several instances of overlap. While Charles had created diversity in his portfolio, he didn't account for overlap in the companies in which the funds were invested. Out of the 36 funds Charles owned, the advisor found 15 that contained identical stocks. While most of the companies were good quality, the high instance of overlap did not contribute to the diversity that Charles wanted and expected. The advisor also provided him with a report that explained* the concentration ratio of his holdings (noting how much of his portfolio was contained within the top 25 stock holdings), the percentage of his portfolio that each company represented and the portfolio date of his account (when the funds in his portfolio were last updated).

Charles agreed to hire the advisor to manage the portfolio going forward. The advisor consolidated his funds into one investment management strategy. The funds were now being managed by someone Charles believed knew his specific investment goals and needs. Eliminating redundancy and overlap in his portfolio was easy to do but difficult to detect since Charles had multiple funds with a couple different brokerage firms. Charles was now much happier with his overall retirement planning. And he lived happily ever after.

This is Yellow Money at its best!

## AVOIDING EMOTIONAL INVESTING

There's no way around it, people get emotional about their money and for good reason. You've spent your life working for it, exchanging your time and talent for it, and making decisions about how to invest it. You've worried and fretted, maybe even screamed at it from time to time. There is one essential fact about money management: emotions don't cause you to make better investment decisions, they make it worse. Relying on emotion rather than experience, training and natural ability, is one reason the stock market is so volatile at times. The market is driven by two emotions: greed and fear. We buy when we feel greedy and sell when we are fearful. It's no wonder that most investors underperform the stock indices. The indices are static portfolios. There is no emotion in the buying and selling of the stocks in the indices. One of the advantages of Yellow Money is that it is managed by a professional, someone other than yourself, **someone who isn't DUI (driving under the influence) of emotion.**

Professional money managers create requirements for each type of investment in which they put your money. We'll call them "screens." Your money manager will run your holdings through the screens they have created to evaluate different types of investment strategies. A professionally managed account will only have holdings that meet the requirements laid out in the overall management plan that was designed to meet your investment goals. The holdings that don't make it through the screens, the ones that don't contribute to your investment goals, are sold and the proceeds reallocated to investments that your financial professional has determined to be more appropriate.

Different screens apply to different Yellow Money strategies. For example, if one of your goals is growth, which would require taking on more risk, an investment professional would screen for companies that have high rates of revenue and sales growth, high earnings growth, rising profit margins, and innovative products. On the other hand, if you want your portfolio to be used for income, which would call for lower risk and less return, your professional would screen for dividend yield and sector diversification. *Every investor has a different goal, and every goal requires a customized strategy.* A professional will create a portfolio that reflects your investment desires. If some of the current assets you own complement the strategies that your professional recommends, those will likely stay in your portfolio.

Screening your assets removes emotion from the equation. It removes attachment to pet stocks or fund companies. Professionals aren't married to particular stocks or funds. They go by the numbers and see your portfolio through a lens shaped by your retirement goals. Your professional understands your wants and needs and creates an investment strategy that takes your life events and future plans into account. It's an unemotional approach, one that allows you to tap into the tools and resources of a professional who has built a career around successful investing. **Managing money is a full-time job and best left to professionals.**

Removing emotions from investing also allows you to be unaffected by the day-to-day volatility of the market. Your financial professional doesn't ask where the market is going to be in a year, three years or a month from now. If you look at the value of the stock market from the beginning of the twentieth century to today, it has continued to go up. Despite the Great Depression, the 1987 crash and the 2008 collapse, the market, as a whole, trends up. Remember the major market downturn in 2008 when the market lost over 30 percent of its value? Not only did it recover those losses but it has exceeded its 2008 value. Yes, it took five years for it to recover but since the market indices are Red Money, how much better could you have done if you had converted these monies to Yellow Money before 2007? Emotional investing led countless people to sell low as the market went down and buy the same shares back after the market was recovering. That's an expensive way to invest. While you can't afford to lose money that you need in two, three or five years, your Need Later Money has time to grow. A more reliable way to grow it is to make it Yellow.

## CREATING AN INVESTMENT STRATEGY

Just like Janet and Charles, chances are you can benefit from taking a more managed investment approach tailored to your goals. Yellow Money is generally Need Later Money that you want to grow for later use. You can work with your financial advisor to create investments that meet your needs within different timeframes. You may need to rely on some of your Yellow Money in 10, 15 or 20 years, whether for additional income, a large purchase you plan on making or a vacation. A financial professional can help you reallocate the risk of your assets as they grow, helping you lock in your profits and secure a source of income you can depend on later.

So what does a Yellow Money account look like? Here's what it *doesn't* look like: a portfolio with 19 small cap mutual funds, a dozen individual stocks and an assortment of bond accounts. A brokerage account with a hodgepodge of investments, even if goal-oriented, is not a professionally managed account. It's still Red Money. Remember, Yellow Money is a managed account that uses an investment strategy not controlled by emotion. When you look at making investments that will meet your future income needs, the burning question becomes: How much should you have in the market and how should it be invested? Following the concepts discussed thus far in this book will help you better allocate your portfolio. Utilizing the help of a professional in this process should help reduce risk and increase the performance of your retirement assets.

## WHY YELLOW MONEY?

If you have already met your immediate income needs for retirement, why bother with a professional money manager? The money you have accumulated above and beyond your income needs may have a greater purpose. Do you have children, grandchildren or siblings you want to bless in the future? Do you have a church or charity that you admire or to which you have given service? Are there other people you know who could just use a break in this life? In short, do you want to craft a legacy? Would you like this legacy left to chance or your own ability to manage the money (review the story of Bill and Mary in the Introduction to this book)? Or would it make more sense to use the help of a professional in managing your entire life's savings?

Utilizing Yellow Money also means that you don't have to burden yourself with the time commitment, the stress and the cost of determining how to manage your money. Yellow Money can help you better enjoy your retirement. Do you want to sit down in your home office every day and determine how to best allocate your assets? Or would you prefer to be living your life while a professional manages your money for you? It's your retirement.

## SEEKING FINANCIAL ADVICE: STOCK BROKERS VS. INVESTMENT ADVISOR REPRESENTATIVES

Investors basically have access to two types of advisors in today's financial world: commission-based stock brokers, sometimes referred to as financial advisors, and fee-based registered investment advisor representatives, who I'll refer to as investment advisors. Most investors, however, don't know the difference between these types of advisors or even that a difference exists. Although I will address this topic in greater detail in Chapter 14, a brief summary may be helpful here.

In a survey taken by TD Ameritrade,* the top reasons investors choose to work with an independent registered investment advisor are:

- Registered Investment Advisors are required, as fiduciaries, to offer advice that is in the best interest of clients
- More personalized service and competitive fee structure offered at a Registered Investment Advisor firm
- Dissatisfaction with full commission brokers

The truth is that there is a difference between stock brokers and investment advisors. Investment advisors are obligated to act in an investor's best interests in all aspects of a financial relationship. Although some stock brokers and financial advisors maintain this standard in their dealings with their clients, they are not under the same obligation to do so.

Here is some information that may help you better understand the differences:

- Investment advisor representatives have the fiduciary duty to act in a client's best interest at all times and with every investment decision they make. Stock brokers and broker-

---

*2011 Advisor Sentiment Study, commissioned by TD AMERITRADE. TD Ameritrade, Inc.

age firms usually do not act as fiduciaries to their clients and are not obligated to follow this standard.

- Investment advisors are required to give their clients a Form ADV describing the methods that the advisor uses to do business as well as a personal profile of the advisor. An Investment Advisor also obtains client consent regarding any conflicts of interest that could exist with the business of the advisor.
- Stock brokers and brokerage firms are not obligated to provide comparable types of disclosure to their customers.
- While stock brokers routinely earn profits by trading as a principal with customers, Investment Advisors do not trade with clients as a principal (except in very limited and specific circumstances).
- Investment Advisors charge a pre-negotiated fee in advance of any transaction. They cannot earn additional profits or commissions from their customers' investments without prior consent. Investment Advisors are commonly paid an asset-based fee that aligns their interests with those of the client. Brokerage firms and stock brokers, on the other hand, have much different payment agreements. Their revenues may increase regardless of the performance of their customers' assets.
- Investment advisors, unlike brokerage firms, do not engage in investment banking or underwriting of securities.

## CHAPTER 3 RECAP //

- There are three types of money: Green, Yellow and Red.
- Green money is safe money, money with guarantees. There are two types of Green Money: **Need Now** and **Need Later**.
- Yellow Money is money that is professionally managed. It has a cohesive purpose and a strategy behind it, usually aimed at reducing risk. It is managed without emotion.
- Red Money is unmanaged money, emotional money. This is the riskiest type of money and is the most unreliable for retirement planning purposes.
- There are big differences between a stock broker or financial advisor and a registered Investment Advisor representative (Investment Advisor).Make sure you know the differences.
- The deck is stacked against the ordinary investor. According to the DALBAR report, individual investors consistently underperform compared to the market because of a variety of factors, including emotional investing.

# 4

# THE RETIREMENT INCOME CHALLENGE

*Opportunity is a haughty goddess who wastes no time with those who are unprepared.*
*— George Clason,* **The Richest Man In Babylon**

A May 13, 2013 **Time.com** article shouted the headline: **The New Retirement: Forget About Being Rich, All We Want Is Peace of Mind**. The article went on to say that by a margin of seven to one, adults over the age of 45 say their focus is on peace of mind, not wealth accumulation, according to a new study from Merrill Lynch and Age Wave. "Today's retirees and pre-retirees crave the peace of mind that comes from having enough money safely tucked away to provide a sufficient and dependable income stream. In the survey, guaranteed income and protecting assets were four times more important than achieving high-risk returns."

The results of this survey may or may not reflect your particular feelings about retirement but it's important to know how your peers feel about it. It's certainly vital for financial professionals to know how clients feel. Regardless of your views, an essential element of any retirement plan is the evaluation of your income needs. Whether you are already retired or still working, finding the most efficient and reliable way to address those needs will have a positive impact on your lifestyle, your asset accumulation and your legacy. Once you've identified your income needs, you will then know how much is left over for Yellow or Red Money investments, which we'll address later.

*Every plan should regularly reassess the expected day-to-day income needs of retirement.* The moment your working income ceases is referred to as the **retirement cliff**. The chasm you face at that moment is both overwhelming and terrifying. What bridges that chasm and allows you to travel across safely to the land of milk, honey and golf is income. When you begin drawing income from your retirement assets, you have entered the distribution phase of your planning. This is where your Green Money, the safer, more reliable assets that you have accumulated just for this purpose, comes into play to provide you with a steady, reliable income.

To satisfy that need for income, you'll first want to determine *how much you'll need* and *when you will need it.*

**How Much Income Will You Need?** It all depends. Will your home be paid for by then? Will you have a vacation home to pay for? Do you plan to travel a lot? Are you in unstable health that may require medical expenses above and beyond what is covered by Medicare? Do you expect to be caring for a needy child or parent during your retirement? These issues and more will affect the amount of income you'll want to plan for.

While this amount will be different for everyone, the general rule of thumb is that a retiree will require 70 to 80 percent of their pre-retirement income to maintain their current lifestyle. Once you've determined that number, the key is to match that expected income need with the best investment strategies to optimize the result. Your Green Money – pensions and social security – will most likely provide most or all of the expected income need. Any shortfall can be assured with lifetime payments from a fixed annuity (see Chapter 6).

## TAKING WITHDRAWALS

For those who prefer to maintain income portfolios chocked full of Yellow and Red Money in place of Green Money, "may the Force be with you." You're asking for quite a challenge in the years ahead. Taking income from a stock and bond portfolio is a tricky thing and not for the faint of heart.

So how much income can you reasonably take from a stock and bond portfolio without later on running out of money? A standard rule used by many financial professionals is the 4 percent income theory. This theory, postulated in the mid-1990s by William Bengen, states that if you hold a portfolio of 50 percent stock and 50 percent bonds and take 4 percent income (adjusted for inflation), there is a 90 percent chance that the portfolio will last 30 years or longer. In other words, there's a 10 percent chance it won't last. OK, that's fairly reliable. There are a lot of people willing to take that bet. So is this a sound assumption to make during retirement? I wouldn't make that assumption for several reasons.

First, recent studies by other researchers, including Nobel Laureate William Sharpe, have debunked the 4 percent income theory as obsolete. Using a more current economic climate rather than the mid-1990s, the 4 percent rule would have a failure rate of 57 percent. A 2013 study by Dr. Wade Pfau concluded that a more reliable combination of investment products for income withdrawals would be a mix of stocks and fixed annuities.

A lot has changed since the mid-1990s. A lot will change going forward. The old market theories will most likely not work well, if at all, going forward. Why? What is the most important number in finance? It's not 4 percent. It's 76 million. As I explained previously, the Boomers have changed everything for at least the next 20 years.

Another reason the 4 percent theory is under scrutiny is because of the use of averages. The use of averages to project the future value of a fluctuating asset may get you a warm and fuzzy number to frame on the wall, but it will seldom be correct. **When you start taking income from a fluctuating investment like a stock portfolio, using an average rate of return in the projections will seldom be correct.** Let me give you an example. If an investment gains 50 percent one year but then loses 50 percent the next year, what is the average rate of return?

Zero, right?

Wrong!

Now let's use real money. A $100 deposit earns $50 the first year leaving you with $150. The $150 loses 50 percent or $75 the next year leaving you with $75. How could you lose 25 percent of your original investment when the average rate of return was supposed to be 0? How did this happen, you ask? Each time the fluctuating asset declines in value, you are compounding the loss by losing some of the previous years' gain. Averaging doesn't take this into account.

This is the fallacy of using average rates of return to project the performance of fluctuating investments. All financial firms use them. Averaging is standard operating procedure. But how many of those firms ever told you that using average rates of return on fluctuating investments is usually meaningless?

This is why it's so important to follow these two rules:

1. Don't lose money.
2. Never forget Rule #1.

Green money is looking a little more attractive, isn't it?

## INSURED WITHDRAWALS VS UNINSURED WITHDRAWALS

What I'm about to show you will test the faith of even the most devout stock market investor, but the results speak for themselves.

Let's say you retired back in September of 1998 and you had a portfolio exceeding $1 million at the time. You decided to split your portfolio among two different assets to diversify the risk. You placed $500,000 in an S&P 500 index fund and another $500,000 in a fixed indexed annuity (FIA) using an S&P 500 Strategy with annual reset. You instructed each account to send you an income check for $25,000 each year on the same day. Fifteen years later, on October 1, 2013, you compared the results. Here's how it turned out:

| Date | S&P 500 | S&P 500 percent change | Account Value | Income | Net Value |
|---|---|---|---|---|---|
| 10/1/2002 | $100,000 | | $500,000 | | |
| 10/1/2003 | $120,909 | 20.91% | $604,545 | ($25,000) | $579,545 |
| 10/1/2004 | $136,937 | 13.26% | $656,371 | ($25,000) | $631,371 |
| 10/1/2005 | $99,228 | -27.54% | $457,507 | ($25,000) | $432,507 |
| 10/1/2006 | $78,869 | -20.52% | $343,768 | ($25,000) | $318,768 |
| 10/1/2007 | $95,952 | 21.66% | $387,813 | ($25,000) | $362,813 |
| 10/1/2008 | $106,268 | 10.75% | $401,820 | ($25,000) | $376,820 |
| 10/1/2009 | $117,033 | 10.13% | $414,992 | ($25,000) | $389,992 |
| 10/1/2010 | $127,344 | 8.81% | $424,352 | ($25,000) | $399,352 |
| 10/1/2011 | $145,542 | 14.29% | $456,421 | ($25,000) | $431,421 |
| 10/1/2012 | $111,033 | -23.71% | $329,128 | ($25,000) | $304,128 |
| 10/1/2013 | $100,770 | -9.24% | $276,017 | ($25,000) | $251,017 |
| 10/1/2014 | $108,789 | 7.96% | $270,992 | ($25,000) | $245,992 |
| 10/1/2015 | $107,857 | -0.86% | $243,884 | ($25,000) | $218,884 |
| 10/1/2016 | $137,337 | 27.33% | $278,711 | ($25,000) | $253,711 |
| 10/1/2017 | $160,300 | 16.72% | $296,132 | ($25,000) | $271,132 |

Total W/Ds ($375,000)

| Date | *FIA percent | Value | Income | Net Value |
|---|---|---|---|---|
| 10/1/2002 | | $500,000 | | |
| 10/1/2003 | 15.09% | $575,450 | ($25,000) | $550,450 |
| 10/1/2004 | 8.68% | $598,230 | ($25,000) | $573,230 |
| 10/1/2005 | 0.00% | $573,230 | ($25,000) | $548,230 |
| 10/1/2006 | 0.06% | $548,559 | ($25,000) | $523,559 |
| 10/1/2007 | 7.79% | $564,329 | ($25,000) | $539,329 |
| 10/1/2008 | 4.47% | $563,433 | ($25,000) | $538,433 |
| 10/1/2009 | 3.42% | $556,844 | ($25,000) | $531,844 |
| 10/1/2010 | 2.34% | $544,291 | ($25,000) | $519,291 |
| 10/1/2011 | 5.16% | $546,087 | ($25,000) | $521,087 |
| 10/1/2012 | 0.00% | $521,087 | ($25,000) | $496,087 |
| 10/1/2013 | 0.00% | $496,087 | ($25,000) | $471,087 |
| 10/1/2014 | 2.48% | $482,770 | ($25,000) | $457,770 |
| 10/1/2015 | 6.62% | $488,073 | ($25,000) | $463,073 |
| 10/1/2016 | 11.48% | $516,233 | ($25,000) | $491,233 |
| 10/1/2017 | 4.01% | $510,933 | ($25,000) | $485,933 |
| | | Total W/Ds | ($375,000) | |
| | Total Benefit- S&P 500 | $646,132 | | |
| | Total Benefit -FIA | $860,933 | | |
| | Difference | $214,801 | 33.24% | |

Once withdrawals entered the picture, the fixed indexed annuity was a far better instrument for income withdrawals over the period of 1998 to 2013 than the S&P 500 index. Even adding the S&P 500 dividends would not have affected the numbers that much. How did this happen? Simple. When the withdrawals were taken from the FIA in the years the S&P 500 lost value, those withdrawals did not compound the loss that year because there never was a loss. By eliminating market losses, the indexed annuity never had to play catch-up. You don't have to earn all the market gains each year to outperform the market if you can

*Performances quoted are approximate and were provided by reliable sources. They do not indicate or guarantee future results.*

eliminate the losses. This is what most money managers try to accomplish for you in a Yellow account.

Of course, past performance is not indicative of future performance. But if I were a betting man, I'd wager that in the next fifteen years the FIA will deliver an impressive withdrawal record compared to the S&P 500 index.

The conclusion? If you want to enjoy a more dependable income during your retirement years, utilize more Green Money. Your portfolio may not grow as much but there's less chance that you'll live longer than expected and be forced to spend your final years living with one of your children.

**When Will You Need It?** The obvious answer to this question is when you retire, but there is more to the answer.

Most people think that when they stop working, it's now time to file for social security and take the company pension. This may not be the best decision, especially if you have other options. Taking social security, for instance, would be a necessity if it was the bulk or all of your retirement income. But if you have other assets or a pension that could be used to pay the bills, you would be rewarded for delaying the social security decision. This is one of the few places where procrastination is rewarded. Every year you wait to receive social security once you're eligible, the government boosts the final paycheck (up to age 70). For life! If your other assets are not guaranteed to earn what social security will pay per year if you wait, it may be advantageous to withdraw from the other assets first.

Another factor that will determine when you take retirement income may be the condition of the stock market at the time. Referring back to the market collapse of 2008, a sizable loss in the value of 401(k) plans, IRAs and other stock accounts caused many people to delay retirement. Obviously, these investors had the luxury of being able to keep their current jobs, which was fortunate for them. Following The Rule of 100 could have prevented some of their losses and allowed them to keep their retirement date. Deciding to own more Yellow Money and less Red Money could have also kept them on schedule for timely retirement.

Another factor in the timing of this decision could be a working spouse or partner. Some couples have the luxury of dual incomes. One may decide to retire and begin taking some form of income while the other continues to work. This benefits both partners. The retired one takes a lesser amount of income from the portfolio, which allows increased growth on the balance. The working partner is bringing in an income which allows the portfolio and social security benefits to grow until needed. This can be a valuable planning option if you're fortunate enough to have a partner who will continue employment.

It is difficult to project exactly when it will be best to begin retirement income. Willingness to adjust to changes in the investment environment as well as in your personal situation can prove to be very beneficial financially.

**What if you're already retired?** It's just as important to regularly reevaluate your current income as it is for pre-retirees to plan for income. Just because you're already retired and receiving income does not mean you cannot benefit from applying these principles to improve that income. The greatest challenge many retirees face is complacency. As long as money keeps showing up in the bank account every month, why worry? The adages, "If I don't change anything, I won't make a mistake" or "If it ain't broke, don't fix it" may make clever conversation, but they are dangerous financial philosophies. Too many of us think that as long as the car is running, we don't need to do any preventive maintenance. Reevaluating your entire portfolio using the principles in this book could be time well spent. Maintaining the status quo could be money well lost. Remember, the game has changed now. So should your thinking and your planning.

## CHAPTER 4 RECAP //

- A successful retirement strategy depends on knowing how much money you need and when you need it. Regularly assess your portfolio and income needs and make necessary adjustments.
- Using an average rate of return to make long-term projections is often meaningless.
- Taking income from a fluctuating investment compounds the losses in the loosing years.
- When it comes to money, remember Buffet's Rules:
- Never lose money
- Never forget Rule #1.

*5*

# UNDERSTANDING SOCIAL SECURITY

*"Be thankful we're not getting all the government we're paying for."*
Will Rogers

The single most important source of retirement income for most Americans is social security. Over 90 percent of us receive or will receive this social benefit. It is the most trusted of all the government programs and the most highly rated for customer satisfaction. If properly utilized, social security can be a valuable and needed tool in retirement planning. In spite of this, the program is on a weak foundation that is projected to run short of money in 15 to 20 years. Attempts have been made by the Boomers, the future recipients, to overhaul the program but politics and a lack of will have stymied any agreement on a plausible solution. To better understand the program and its challenges, let's go back to the beginning.

## ROOSEVELT'S NEW DEAL

In 1935, America was struggling to cope with the effects of The Depression with its high unemployment rate, high poverty rate and lack of social programs for its citizens. As one of his initiatives to revitalize the nation, President Roosevelt established the Social Security Administration as a safety net for seniors. Roosevelt modeled the program after a similar program already established in Germany many years before.

The system would require American workers to contribute taxes from their paychecks to fund the program. The taxes would be collected and sent to a special trust fund where the benefit checks would be disbursed to those who qualified. The first payment from the system was given in 1940 to a woman named Ida Mae Fuller. Up to that time, she had contributed only $23 to the program. By the time she died, she received nearly $22,000 in benefits. This was just the beginning of the troubles for America's most beloved social program.

The program worked pretty well in the beginning. There were far more workers contributing to the trust fund than senior citizens receiving payments, which offset the low contribution of the seniors receiving benefits. Even as late as 1950, there were 16 workers for every retiree so there was plenty of inflow against the outflow. What also made the program work was that the average life expectancy in 1935 was 65 years, so seniors didn't receive benefits for very long, if at all.

Over time the demographics began changing and the health of the program became suspect. Beginning after WWII, the Boomers entered the picture, which injected a huge surge of potential recipients into the system. In addition, medical breakthroughs have extended life expectancy so people are living longer and taking more out of the system. To complicate matters, the Boomers didn't have very many children to replace themselves in the workforce. This would explain why there are only 3.3 workers per retiree today and that number will decrease as the Boomers retire. This will create a huge funding problem in the middle of the Boomer retirement cycle – more outflow than inflow.

David Walker, former Comptroller of the United States, described the program's troubles this way, "The truth is that the government's Social Security guarantee is one huge unfunded promise." Speaking of the payroll taxes that are collected, he continues, "All this money is transmitted to the federal government and credited to the Social Security trust funds... However, rather than saving the money and investing it in a diversified pool of real and readily marketable assets, the government spends it and provides "special-issue" government securities in return" (**Come Back America,** p. 70).

It's no wonder the integrity of the program is in jeopardy.

It's important to note that social security was never intended to be the sole income support for Americans after retirement. It was not designed this way, however, social security has become the sole source of income for many retirees.

In spite of these challenges, I am confident that social security will be rescued and that it can be relied upon as an income source during retirement for the Boomers. For their children and grand-children? I'm not as confident.

## HOW DOES SOCIAL SECURITY WORK?

*Mary had worked full-time nearly her entire adult life and was looking forward to enjoying retirement with her husband, kids and grandkids. When she turned 62, she decided to take advantage of her social security benefit as soon as it became available.*

*A couple of years later, while organizing some paperwork in her home office, she came across an old social security statement. As she reviewed the statement, she realized that she might have been better off waiting to file for benefits. She had enough money in her portfolio at the time to delay the social security decision. There were just too many pressing issues at the time to study all the ramifications of a social security decision.*

Mary made a note to call the Social Security Administration to see if it was possible to change her monthly benefit to a larger amount. She was told she could not change her decision because she was beyond the one-year time limit to make changes.

Here are some facts that illustrate how Americans currently use social security:

- 90 percent of Americans age 65 and older receive social security benefits.[*]
- Social security provides 39 percent of income for retired Americans.[*]
- Claiming social security benefits at the wrong time can reduce your monthly benefit by up to 57 percent.[**]
- 43 percent of men and 48 percent of women claim social security benefits at age 62.[**]
- 74 percent of retirees receive reduced social security benefits.[**]
- In 2013, the average monthly social security benefit was $1,261. *The maximum benefit for 2013 was $2533.*[***]

There are some aspects of social security that are well known but many others that are not. Social Security is a massive government program that rivals anything in the private sector. You don't have to understand all of the intricacies of social security to maximize

---

[*]*http://www.ssa.gov/pressoffice/basicfact.htm*

[**]*When to Claim Social Security Benefits, David Blanchett, CFA, CFP® January, 2013*

[***]*http://www.socialsecurity.gov/pressoffice/factsheets/colafacts2013.com*

its advantages. You simply need to find the right professional who can coordinate your other retirement plans with the social security decision so as to maximize the benefits of each. Knowing your options and knowing the right time to file for those options can be worth the price of good advice. Unfortunately, the Social Security Administration, as helpful as they are, will not show you how to maximize your benefit. They are not in the business of retirement planning.

There are many aspects of social security that you have no control over. You don't control how much you put into it nor what it's invested in nor how the government manages it. However, you do control when and how you file for benefits. The most commonly asked question regarding social security is, "When should I file for benefits?" There are some key pieces of information you'll need to know before answering this question.

Before we get into a few calculations and strategies, let's start by covering the basic information about social security. Just as the foundation of a house creates the stable platform for the rest of the framework to rest upon, your social security benefit is an integral part of your overall retirement plan. The purpose of the information that follows is not to give an exhaustive explanation of how social security works, but to maybe clarify some information you already know.

Let's start with eligibility.

**Eligibility.** To receive retirement benefits from social security, you must earn eligibility. In almost all cases, Americans born after 1929 must earn 40 quarters of credit to be eligible to file for retirement benefits. In 2013, a social security credit represents $1,160 of earned income in a calendar quarter. The number changes each year since it is indexed for inflation. Four quarters of credit is the maximum number of credits that can be earned each year. In 2013, you would have had to earn at least $4,640 to accumulate four credits. Although there may be cost of living adjustments made, you are locked into that base benefit amount forever.

**Primary Insurance Amount.** This represents the amount of your benefit at your Full Retirement Age (FRA). All benefit calculations for either early or delayed retirement utilize this number. If you opt to take benefits before your FRA, your monthly benefit will be less than your PIA. If you delay filing for benefits, your PIA will increase but only until age 70. After age 70, there will be no further increase in your PIA if you delay filing for benefits.

**Full Retirement Age.** Your FRA is an important factor for determining your social security benefits. Your FRA is dictated by your year of birth and is the age at which you can begin your full monthly benefit (PIA).

| Year of Birth | Full Retirement Age |
| --- | --- |
| 1943-1954 | 66 |
| 1955 | 66 and 2 months |
| 1956 | 66 and 4 months |
| 1957 | 66 and 6 months |
| 1958 | 66 and 8 months |
| 1959 | 66 and 10 months |
| 1960 or later | age 67 |

When Social Security was initially established, the FRA was 65 and it still is for people born before 1938. Over time, adjustments to the system have increased the age at which you are eligible to receive your PIA. If you were born between 1938 and 1960, your full retirement age is somewhere on a sliding scale between 65 and 67. Anyone born in 1960 or later will now have to wait until age 67 for full benefits. Increasing the FRA has helped the government reduce the cost of the Social Security program, which pays out more than half a trillion dollars to beneficiaries every year!*

*A Social Security Owner's Manual, Blankenship, 2013; Social Security Administration*

While you can begin collecting benefits as early as age 62, you will receive less than your PIA for filing early. It is important to remember that filing for benefits before your FRA will result in a *reduction to your monthly benefit that remains in place for the rest of your life.* You can also delay receiving benefits up to age 70, in which case your benefits will be higher than your PIA for the rest of your life.

## ROLL UP YOUR SOCIAL SECURITY

Your social security income "rolls up" the longer you wait to claim it. Your monthly benefit will continue to increase until you turn age 70. Because social security is the primary source of income for most retirees, many feel they don't have control over how or when they receive their benefits. This might explain why 74 percent of retirees receive reduced benefits. They filed early. As a matter of fact, only 4 percent of Americans wait until **after** their FRA to file for benefits! This is an alarming trend, despite the fact that the government will increase your benefit if you delay. An often overlooked truth about social security is that every dollar you increase your benefit means less money you will have to withdraw from your nest egg to meet your retirement income needs! That means a greater legacy to pass on to the ones you love. For most Americans, social security is the most important decision they can make to positively impact the rest of their retired lives. *The difference between the best and worst social security decision can be tens of thousands of dollars over a lifetime – over $200,000 of forfeited benefits!*

## DECIDING NOW OR LATER:

Following the above logic, it makes sense to wait as long as you can to begin receiving your social security benefit. However, the decision isn't always that simple. Not everyone has the luxury of waiting. As was mentioned previously *nearly 50 percent of*

*62-year-old Americans file for social security benefits.* Why is this number so high? Some want to retire now and have no other income options. Others might be in poor health and don't feel they will live long enough to justify delaying to file. It is also possible, however, that the majority filing early for benefits are simply under-informed about the advantages of waiting. They may not have coordinated their other retirement plans with the social security decision to maximize the potential of both assets. Regardless of the reasons, you will want to consider the following before making your decision:

File Immediately if You:
- Find your job is unbearable.
- Are willing to sacrifice retirement income.
- Are not healthy and need a reliable source of income.

Consider Delaying Your Benefit if You:
- Want to maximize your retirement income.
- Want to increase retirement benefits for your spouse.
- Are still working and enjoy it.
- Are healthy and willing / able to wait to file.
- Want your spouse to take a percentage of your benefit (you must be married for at least 10 years to receive spousal benefits).

If you decide to wait, how long should you wait? Some people can delay the decision a year or two but not everyone can wait until they are 70 years old. If you do the math, you will see that between ages 62 and 70, there are 96 months in which you can file for social security. If your spouse is the same age, they have 96 months. Add in the various filing options that you're both eligible for, and you can easily end up with more than 20,000 different calculations. This isn't the kind of math that most people would do. Each month would result in a different benefit amount based on the filing options chosen. The longer you wait, the higher your monthly benefit amount becomes.

*The best choice is to maximize your lifetime benefits.* That may not always mean waiting until age 70, when you can "roll up" to the largest monthly payment. To maximize your benefit, you want to find out how to get the most money out of social security over the number of years that you draw from it. As I mentioned previously, the difference between the BEST and WORST social security elections can result in over $200,000 in lost benefits.

If you understand that every month you delay your social security benefit will increase but that delaying also reduces the number of benefit checks you'll receive overall, how are you gaining by delaying? The answer is that for every person there is an age "sweet spot." Filing for the right options at the right time can maximize your benefit over your lifetime *if* you live to average life expectancy. Of course, your life expectancy is impossible to predict with accuracy but you can make an educated guess based on family history, current health and habits.

Financial professionals have access to software that can calculate the best year and month for you to file for benefits based on your life expectancy. You can customize the input by estimating your life expectancy based on your health, habits and family history. *You have much more personal information about these things than the government does.* This will put you in the driver's seat to get the most out of social security based on **your** life expectancy instead of the government table. Getting the highest possible benefit from the program decreases the withdrawals needed from other sources.

## CASE STUDY

*John and Mary Doe are a typical American couple with a 401(k), an IRA and some CDs that total about $400,000. John is 55 years* *old and Mary is 52. They want to retire at age 62 but are open to working longer if it makes sense financially and they stay healthy. They decided to work with a retirement professional to make sure they would avoid a regrettable decision. Since they did not have current social security statements, the advisor helped them log on to the Social Security website (ssa.gov) to retrieve their social security information.*

*The website showed John's projected PIA was $2,507 a month and Mary's was $1,097. If they filed at age 62 for social security, their combined monthly benefits would be $2,451 a month. The expected lifetime benefits would total $567,675, assuming they both live to the average life expectancy. Neither of them had a pension. Their goal was to retire with a monthly income of $5,000. To make up the shortfall, John and Mary would have to rely on withdrawals of over $2,500 a month from their other assets.*

*After running a Social Security Maximization Report on the computer, the advisor was able to show John and Mary their particular "sweet spot." If they waited until John reached age 67 and then they both file using a combination of the Spousal Benefit, Restricted Application and Retired Worker Benefit, they increased their monthly benefit amount to $4,352. Their expected lifetime benefits could be $802,903. This increased their total payments from social security by a whopping **$235,228!** John and Mary were very surprised by the new information and decided to delay retirement. The choice to work with a retirement professional rather than planning their own retirement paid handsomely in additional dollars for retirement.*

As discussed previously, maximizing your benefit involves more than just waiting until age 70 for your maximum monthly benefit amount. The three most common ages related to social security benefits are age 62, age 66, and age 70. In almost all circumstances, filing for benefits at any of these three ages will **not** provide you the maximum lifetime benefit.

Obtaining the proper advice regarding your elections and the timing of social security benefits is a valuable choice in the retirement planning process. Before you pick up the phone and call the Social Security Administration, you should know that the SSA representatives are actually prohibited from giving you election advice! In addition, SSA representatives in general are trained to focus on monthly benefit amounts, not lifetime benefit totals for a couple or family. A retirement professional is your best choice for advice in this area. They can generate a Maximization Report that represents an invaluable resource for understanding your options and the timing of those options.

## SOCIAL SECURITY BENEFIT OPTIONS

- **Retired Worker Benefit.** This is the benefit with which most people are familiar. It is your benefit based on your earnings and the amount that you have paid into the system over the span of your career.
- **Spousal Benefit.** The Spousal Benefit is available to the spouse of someone who is eligible for Retired Worker Benefits, even if that spouse had no earnings. Once the working spouse files for his or her benefit, the other spouse can also file to receive up to half of the working spouse's benefit. If both spouses qualify for social security, one can file for Retired Worker Benefits while the other files for Spousal Benefits. This will allow the latter spouse's benefit to roll up for a few more years until needed.
- **Survivorship Benefit.** When one spouse passes away, the survivor is able to receive the larger of the deceased spouse's benefit or their own benefit. You can apply as early as age 60 but the benefit will be reduced.
- **File and Suspend**. This concept allows for a lower-earning spouse to receive up to 50 percent of the other spouses' PIA amount if both spouses file for benefits at the right time.

- **Restricted Application**. A higher-earning spouse may be able to start collecting a spousal benefit on the lower-earning spouse's benefit while allowing his or her benefit to continue to grow.

## DIVORCED

A divorced spouse can receive benefits from a former spouse's social security record if he or she:

- Was married to the former spouse for at least 10 years
- Is at least age 62 years old
- Is unmarried
- Is not entitled to a higher social security benefit on his or her own record

## WORKING IN RETIREMENT

You can receive a social security benefit while you continue to work but the benefit will be reduced if:

- You're under your Full Retirement Age (FRA)
- You earn more than $15,120 in a year (the threshold).
- One dollar of social security benefit will be withheld for every two dollars you earn over the threshold.
- Beginning one year before your FRA, your benefit is reduced by one dollar for every three dollars you earn over the threshold.

## CHAPTER 5 RECAP//

- How can I maximize my lifetime social security benefit? By knowing when and how to file for the right benefit options. This usually means waiting until you have at least reached your Full Retirement Age (FRA).

- By coordinating your social security benefits with your pension, 401(k), IRA or other retirement assets, you are in the best position to maximize the benefits of each asset.
- Who will provide reliable advice for making these decisions? Only a retirement professional has the tools and experience to provide reliable advice in this area. The Social Security Administration does not have the obligation nor the tools to help you maximize your benefits.

# 6

# FILLING THE INCOME GAP

*When a man retires, his wife gets twice the husband but only half the income.*

*— Chi Chi Rodriguez*

You've organized your assets into Green, Yellow and Red Money. You've followed The Rule of 100 to balance the risk in your portfolio and you've determined how and when to file for maximum social security benefits. If you're not retired yet, you've decided whether you will retire early or wait to maximize those benefits. Now we will focus on providing for any income shortfall that may exist between your actual monthly income and your desired monthly income. We call this the **Income Gap.** Even if you're currently retired, you may want or need more income. If you're fortunate enough to own other assets you can draw from, are those assets the best choice to fill any Income Gap? Should they be changed?

As I mentioned previously, taking withdrawals over a long period of time from a fluctuating asset is a risky proposition. You might ask yourself, "If I need more lifetime income, do I want *I Hope So* income or *I Know So* income?" Once you've answered that question, you've narrowed down the choice of investments for the money that will provide that income. If your answer is *I Hope So* income, then a traditional portfolio of stocks, bonds, options or real estate may satisfy you. I'll address "risk in the hope of greater gain" investments in the next couple of chapters. However, if you prefer to generate *I Know So* income – Green income – then your choices are limited to four basic options: cash, FDIC-backed bank accounts, US Government securities or fixed annuities.

The first two, bank accounts and US Government securities, are tied into the interest rate market. Since we are experiencing one of the lowest interest rate environments in history, most of us would agree that these two options are not viable at this time. That leaves fixed annuities. Aren't fixed annuities tied into the interest rate market? Some are, some aren't. It depends on the type of annuity you choose.

Now is a good time to address some of the facts and myths that surround annuities. For some reason, bringing up the topic of annuities is like declaring you're a Democrat at a Republican Convention. It brings out the deepest opinions in people. You either love annuities or hate them or don't know much about them. There is clearly much confusion regarding the viability of annuities in planning. We can thank the clever marketing of competing advisors and financial institutions that don't offer annuities for creating most of this confusion. Regardless of your position, let's set the record straight.

## ANNUITIES

Annuities are tax-deferred time deposits with a life insurance company. There are two major categories of annuities: immediate annuities and deferred annuities.

## SINGLE PREMIUM IMMEDIATE ANNUITIES (SPIA)

A single premium immediate annuity is simply a contract between you and an insurance company to provide guaranteed stream of payments over a specified time period. That time period could be five, 10 or 15 years or for your life. In other words, you're turning the deposit into a promise of payments over time. The insurance company guarantees or insures that the payments will be sent. Guarantees from a life insurance company are based on the claims-paying ability of the issuing insurance company. Once the time period expires, that's it. No money is left. Zilch! Nada! The insurance company met its obligation to you. These types of annuities are not the best choice if you pass away too soon or if you intended to pass on the remainder to loved ones.

SPIAs provide investors with a stream of reliable income when they can't afford to take the risk of losing money in a fluctuating market. There is a general acceptance that the market always trends up, at least in the long-term. But if you're focusing on income over a shorter period of time, you may not be able to absorb a big hit in the market. Beyond normal market volatility, interest rates also come with an inherent level of uncertainty, making it hard to create a dependable income on your own. SPIAs help remove these concerns. SPIAs used to be the backbone of the retirement planning industry. With the creation of new annuity products, however, they are used much less today than in the past.

## DEFERRED ANNUITIES

Deferred annuities are deposits in which the goal is to defer the income choice until a later time (or indefinitely) while you increase the assets and enjoy tax deferral in the process. There are two main types of deferred annuities: variable and fixed.

**Variable** annuities allow you to invest your monies in a selection of funds called sub-accounts. These sub-accounts are similar to mutual funds, which means you are taking the market risk on the performance of your account balance. Variable annuities are the most expensive annuity policies to own. Policy fees can run up to 3 percent a year, based on the riders chosen. Variable annuities can contain some guarantees but they are classified as Red Money even though they can have some Green Money components (some guarantees). You would choose a variable annuity when you're wanting to take "risk in the hope of greater gain."

**Fixed** annuities, however, are guaranteed contracts with the insurance company. There are many types of fixed annuities but the only type I will describe here is the indexed annuity. It is my favorite annuity choice for use in retirement planning these days. Like any investment choice, indexed annuities may or may not be the best choice for you. It's always best to consult a financial professional **who is well versed in all types of annuities** to help you decide which one, if any, are suitable for you.

## TAKING THE HYBRID APPROACH

**Indexed** annuities are a hybrid approach to the annuity arena. What if you could enjoy some of the best features of both a variable annuity and a fixed annuity? In other words, what if you could get some stock market gains without the risk of losing your money when the market falls? Enter the indexed annuity. Initially created in the mid-1990s, indexed annuities have grown increasingly popular since that time.

One of the most attractive features of this Green Money asset is something called "annual reset." This feature provides possible interest credits based on the performance of one or more of the index crediting methods that you've chosen. These crediting methods are based on the performance of one of the market in-dices, usually the S&P 500 index. If the market goes up during your anniversary year, you are credited with an interest gain based on the cap and participation rate of your contract. If the index declines during the next year, you lose nothing. Your account value stays the same and you simply reset for the next year. I call it the "stairway to heaven." Each year, like a stairway, you either step up or stay level. You never retreat or play catch-up. This makes for a more reliable option to plan a retirement income or a legacy.

In order for an insurance company to be able to provide the guarantees on an indexed annuity contract, the companies estab-lish surrender periods and surrender charges. If you remove your money from the annuity contract during the surrender period, you will pay a surrender charge on the amount withdrawn that exceeds 10 percent of the account value. Most annuities allow a 10 percent penalty-free withdrawal each year. A typical surrender period is 10 years. If during the first ten years you decide you want all your money back, you will pay a declining penalty on the withdrawal.

During the surrender period, an annuity is not a demand deposit account like a savings or checking account. It is a *Need Later* asset. This is why it is essential that you maintain a reserve fund and other liquid funds in addition to your "time deposit" in any annuity.

## INCOME RIDER

Another vital feature of an indexed annuity is an income rider. An income rider is a valuable benefit that allows lifetime income withdrawals (as opposed to annuitizing) when you decide to ex-ercise the rider. While you are waiting to take the income, your income account value (IAV) increases by a fixed rate, somewhere between 4 percent and 7 percent, depending on the contract. Es-sentially, this IAV rate is a back-up, for income purposes only, in case the strategies (the market indexes) don't perform well. Having a minimum rate of interest to project your future income stream is a valuable tool in retirement income planning. It takes a lot of the guesswork out of projections.

The income rider terminates at the death of the annuitant. The rider can continue if the spouse is the sole beneficiary and meets certain conditions, otherwise, the balance of the account value is paid to the designated beneficiaries. This is the biggest advantage of using an income rider – a possible death benefit. There is no death benefit paid when you annuitize an annuity.

To summarize:
- If you are younger and want to structure an annuity investment for growth over a long period of time and you're willing to take the risk, you would select a variable annuity. A variable annuity is Red Money. As the name suggest, it has a variable performance based on investment choices you select. There is no "annual reset" feature which locks in your account gains. You're at the mercy of the market and your ability to manage the market. Policy fees are high but can be worth it if the market performs well. This type of annuity also offers an income rider to structure lifetime income payments. The rider is often exercised when there has been a significant decline in the account value due to market conditions.
- As you approach retirement and begin making adjustments to reduce the Red Money in your portfolio, you might consider a SPIA. A SPIA is an appropriate annuity choice if you want the highest possible lifetime income or you only want income for a stated period of time. SPIAs do not pass on to a beneficiary any remaining funds at your death if you chose the lifetime payout option. This

is seldom the best option for retirees who want to leave a legacy.

- Another option to increase the Green Money in your portfolio is to choose an indexed annuity. Indexed annuities are a type of fixed annuity that offers the potential to earn more interest than other types of fixed annuities or safe alternatives. This is done by choosing an index crediting method based on one of the stock market indexes and utilizing an annual reset feature. Your credited interest each year is never lost due to index declines in the future. You can use an indexed annuity to safely accumulate assets, provide income or both. By exercising an income rider, you will receive lifetime income and any remaining account value at your death will be paid to your beneficiaries. Indexed annuities are better options if you prefer safe accumulation of assets, lifetime income or both, with the remaining balance passed on to your beneficiaries.
- Annuities can work very well to create income. A qualified financial professional can help you find the one that best matches your particular needs.

## CASE STUDY:

*Bob and Mary are both 62 years old. They have determined that they will need $6,000 per month to pay their bills and maintain their current lifestyle in retirement. Their social security benefits will pay them a total of $4,200 per month in benefits at age 66. They also receive $350 per month in rent from a tenant who lives in a small house in their backyard. Between their social security and the monthly rent income, they will be short $1,450 per month.*

*Bob has a 401(k) that is currently worth $375,000. At first glance, it seems that Bob & Mary will have plenty of money. After running some numbers, Bob discovers that since the 401(k) is fully taxable when withdrawn, he'll need to take $1,711 a month to net $1,450* *after taxes. At this withdrawal rate, the 401(k) will most likely run out of money if they live too long. The risk of leaving the money in the market is also not appealing. Bob considers rolling the 401(k) into an IRA at the bank using CDs, but with interest rates so low, CDs are not a viable option. Their pot at the end of the rainbow has become a cup for them. It will not provide what they expected. They must now grapple with the painful issue of figuring out how to lower their expenses and their expectations of retirement. Bob and Mary decide to seek the help of a professional.*

*After reviewing their financial situation, their goals, and their objectives, the financial professional recommends that they rollover $325,000 of the 401(k) into an IRA using an indexed annuity with an income rider to provide the income they need. At age 66, the annuity would guarantee a lifetime income of $1,711 per month that will be needed to meet their retirement goals. Any excess account value remaining at Bob's death would be paid to Mary or the children. This leaves $50,000 to be invested for growth as Need Later money.*

*The cup became a pot again and now a rainbow covers their retirement dreams.*

## CHAPTER 6 RECAP //

- After social security and any other guaranteed income is determined, the amount of income you still lack to meet your needs is called the *Income Gap*.
- Every dollar of increase you can get from social security is less money you'll have to withdraw from your pot of gold to supplement your income needs.
- Annuities are a reliable and predictable way to provide income during retirement. Choosing the right annuity for your situation is essential to achieving your accumulation or income goals.
- Variable annuities may be the best choice for those who are younger and wanting to take risk in the hope of greater gain.
- Indexed annuities may be the better choice for those who desire safety and guaranteed lifetime income. If you don't need income, indexed annuities may still be the better choice for those wanting growth potential without the risk of losing their principle and their gains.
- Be sure you understand the features, benefits, costs and fees associated with any annuity product before you invest.

# 7

# GROWING YOUR ASSETS

*Foul cankering rust the hidden treasure frets,*
*But gold that's put to use more gold begets.*
*— William Shakespeare*

Whether you are 30 years old or 75 years old, the most common question regarding money set aside for the future is: "How do I make it grow?" This question has myriad answers and they all involve some degree of risk. The word "growth" is synonymous with risk, and basically any financial vehicle that isn't Green Money (cash, bank accounts, US Government securities or fixed annuities) is classified as growth money or Red Money. With growth investments, you're taking "risk in the hope of greater gain."

But what about corporate bonds? They're not growth investments, are they? No, corporates are not considered growth vehicles but they're not Green Money either. The standard asset allocation in the securities world usually includes some corporate or municipal bonds in a portfolio, usually for diversification reasons. These instruments are low risk and help reduce the overall risk in a portfolio, but they are not guaranteed against loss. For our purposes, bonds are Red Money, although on the low end of the risk scale. Understanding this principle will assist you in determining how much Green, Yellow and Red Mooney you ought to have in your retirement portfolio before or after you retire.

There are many good books written on the topic of how to be successful in stocks, bonds, commodities or real estate investing. I will not attempt to add to that tome with this book. I will, however, expound briefly on some general concepts that I've learned from some of the best investors and traders in the world as well as from my own experience. These concepts are only the beginning of the knowledge needed to be successful. They are critical to understanding how to "grow" your Yellow or Red Money instead of just planting those monies and hoping for a bountiful harvest.

## MANAGING THE STOCK MARKET

The stock market can send even a seasoned professional into a rage. Every day the market is open the risk of losing money is present. The less you are trained in market behavior the more you are apt to lose at some point. The stock market is no friend to the average investor over the long term, as the next chapter will attest. **Any investor can make money in an up market. The test of investor talent is how well you preserve what you've gained when the market isn't going up.** The problem is not in the stock market. Stocks go up and down. They always have; they always will. The problem is in ourselves, as Benjamin Graham so astutely stated. **Knowing when to buy and when to sell and when to do nothing is as important as what to buy.** All four of these decisions separate great investors from poor investors.

To understand the stock market, it's important to know what drives it. Simply put, the main driver of the stock market is emotion. The market does not act rationally. It is driven by two emotions: fear and greed. Greed causes us to buy. Fear causes us to sell. What gets most investors in trouble is the inability to manage those emotions. They buy when they should be waiting. They sell when they should be buying. Their emotions control their decision-making. Investors who aren't emotional gain at the expense of those who are.

Billionaire Warren Buffet teaches powerful but simple lessons in his annual reports to shareholders. In the 2013 Berkshire Hathaway Report (p. 19), he summed up this issue as follows:

*"Owners of stocks, however, too often let the capricious and often irrational behavior of their fellow owners cause them to behave irrationally as well. Because there is so much chatter about markets, the economy, interest rates, price behavior of stocks, etc., some investors believe it is important to listen to pundits – and worse yet, important to consider acting upon their comments.*

"Those people… too often become frenetic when they are exposed to a stream of stock quotations and accompanying commentators delivering an implied message of 'Don't just sit there, do something.' For these investors, liquidity is transformed from the unqualified benefit it should be to a curse."

I couldn't have said it any better.

**The best investors and traders have a system of trading that they follow**. This removes emotions from the decision-making process, emotions that would otherwise lead to inferior performance. There are a myriad of trading systems, investment newsletters and books you can buy on trading systems. You'll learn a lot about Warren Buffet's system by reading his annual reports to shareholders. These systems involve time, expense and trial-and-error in order to find the one that works best for you. But remember, the game has changed now. Many of the old trading systems and market theories may not work very well, if at all, in the new Boomer retirement world. Finding a successful system that will work in this new environment will be your biggest challenge since it is still evolving.

The easier, more reliable route, is to hire an experienced investment advisor or money manager to manage the money for you. Professionals already have systems in place that they follow. For most people, finding a professional to turn your Red Money into Yellow Money will be the best decision, especially during the retirement years. **Do you really want to spend your retirement days experimenting with your life's savings because you won't trust someone smarter than you?** Unfortunately, many do, and some do well at it but some end up ruining their portfolios and moving in with the kids. Sometimes, I guess, it takes a village to get through retirement.

## THE MATH OF REBOUNDS

The key to successful investing is managing your losses. This is what average investors – emotional investors – don't do very well. Once you incur a loss in a fluctuating investment, playing catch-up is a risky and often costly activity. It all comes down to math but not the kind of math you learned in school. This kind of math is usually learned in the school of hard knocks.

What if I told you that -30 + 43 = 0. Would you believe me? Probably not. You'd wonder where I went to school. The truth is that -30 + 43 actually does equal 0 – when it comes to the math of rebounds. The math is as follows:

$$\$100 - 30 \text{ percent loss } (\$30) = \$70$$
$$\$70 + 43 \text{ percent gain } (\$30) = \$100$$

To emphasize the danger in using Red Money in your retirement plan, let's use another example. Let's assume a $100,000 investment. Which of the following rates of return would you prefer to have during retirement:

| End of Year | Hypothetical Rate | Ending Value |
|:---:|:---:|:---:|
| 1 | 8 percent | $108,000 |
| 2 | 8 percent | $116,640 |
| 3 | -8 percent | $107,308 |
| | **OR** | |
| 1 | 2.8 percent | $102,800 |
| 2 | 2.8 percent | $105,678 |
| 3 | 2.8 percent | $108,637 |

Once again, some Red Money in a portfolio is justified, however, if you want to speculate in the stock market or any other fluctuating market on your own, you'd better know what you're doing. Most investors, I'm convinced, would be better off hiring a professional to manage the money (turning Red Money to Yellow Money). If that isn't going to happen, then they should at least reduce their risk by using more Green Money in the portfolio. It all comes down to being able to manage the losses that will inevitably occur. Or just using the right math.

## CHAPTER 7 RECAP//

- Growth is synonymous with risk. The risk in not in the stocks. The risk in in us.
- Successful investing involves removing emotion from the trading decision. This is best accomplished by using a trading system.
- Managing losses, not stock picking, is the key to successful investing.

# 8

# THE IMPACT OF VOLATILITY ON THE INDIVIDUAL INVESTOR

*If you lend someone $20 and never see them again, it was probably worth it.*

— Unknown author

Lisa's story illustrates how market volatility can have major repercussions for an individual investor.

*Lisa worked for Acme Paper Company for 34 years. During that time, she acquired bonuses in the form of company stock. She also contributed part of her paycheck every month to a 401(k) plan. By the time she retired at age 62, she had $250,000 worth of Acme stock and $250,000 in the 401(k). Lisa retired early because of failing health.*

*Because she retired early, Lisa failed to maximize her social security benefit. Her income needs are $3,500 per month, including taxes. Lisa's monthly social security benefit is $1,900, leaving her with a*

*$1,600 income gap. To fill that gap, Lisa sells $1,600 of Acme stock each month to meet her income needs. She determined that filling the income gap from Acme stock would cost her less tax than taking the withdrawals from her 401(k) plan.*

Unfortunately for Lisa, she retired in 2007, just before the major market correction. She lost more than 20 percent of the value of her Acme stock and over 30 percent of her 401(k) plan in 2008. Because Lisa needed to sell Acme stock each month to meet her income needs, the market value of the stock was secondary to her need for more income. She felt helpless to stem the losses during the 2008 correction.

Lisa has since learned that if she had reallocated her portfolio using The Rule of 100 as a starting point, she could have greatly reduced the risk in her portfolio and avoided much of the loss that she realized in 2008. She also discovered that she could have insured her 401(k) account against any loss while guaranteeing an income of $1600 a month for her lifetime.

In 2013, the well-respected financial services market research firm, DALBAR, released their annual "Quantitative Analysis of Investment Behavior" report (QAIB). The report studied the impact of market volatility on individual investors – people like Lisa who manage their own investments in the stock market.

According to the study, volatility not only caused investors to make decisions based on their emotions, but those decisions often resulted in inferior performance compared to holding those same positions as part of an asset allocation strategy. Why do investors tinker with their stock and bond holdings? Because they do not have a system to follow. They react to the markets instead of act upon them.

DALBAR's "Quantitative Analysis of Investor Behavior" has been used to measure the effects of investor' purchases and mutual fund redemptions since 1994. The QAIB shows that over nearly a 20 year period, the average investor earned less, and in many cases, significantly less, than the performance of the mutual funds they utilized. QAIB's goal is to improve independent investor performance and help financial professionals provide advice that addresses the concerns and behaviors of the average investor.

An excerpt from the report states:

*"QAIB offers guidance on how and where investor behaviors can be improved. No matter what the state of the mutual fund industry, boom or bust: Investment results are more dependent on investor behavior than on fund performance. Mutual fund investors who hold on to their investments are more successful than those who time the market."*

*QAIB uses data from the Investment Company Institute (ICI), Standard & Poor's and Barclays Capital Index Products to compare mutual fund investor returns to an appropriate set of benchmarks.*

*There are actually three primary causes for the chronic shortfall for both equity and fixed-income investors:*

1. *Capital not available to invest. This accounts for 25 percent to 35 percent of the shortfall.*
2. *Capital needed for other purposes. This accounts for 35 percent to 45 percent of the shortfall.*
3. *Psychological factors. These account for 45 percent to 55 percent of the shortfall."*

The key findings of DALBAR's QAIB report shown below provide compelling statistics about how individual investment strategies produced negative outcomes for the majority of investors:

- Psychological factors account for 45 percent to 55 percent of the chronic investment return shortfall for both equity and fixed income investors.

- Asset allocation is designed to handle the investment decision-making for the investor, which can materially reduce the shortfall due to psychological factors.
- Successful asset allocation investing requires investors to act on two critical imperatives:
  a. Balance capital preservation and appreciation so that it is aligned with the investor's objective.
  b. Select a qualified allocator.
- The best way for an investor to determine their risk tolerance is to utilize a risk tolerance assessment. However, these assessments must be accessible and usable.
- Evaluating allocator quality requires analysis of the allocator's underlying investments, decision making process and record of successful outcomes from past efforts.
- Choosing a top allocator makes a significant difference in the investment results one will achieve.
- Mutual fund retention rates suggest that the average investor has not remained invested for long enough to derive the potential benefits of the investment markets.
- Retention rates for asset allocation funds exceed those of equity and fixed income funds by over a year.
- Investors' ability to correctly time the market is highly dependent on the direction of the market. Investors generally guess right more often in up markets. However, in 2012 investors guessed right only 42 percent of the time.
- Analysis of investor fund flows compared to market performance further supports the argument that investors are unsuccessful at timing the market. Market upswings rarely coincide with mutual fund inflows, while market downturns do not coincide with mutual fund outflows.
- Average equity mutual fund investors gained 15.56 percent compared to a gain of 15.98 percent for the S&P 500 index.

- The shortfall in the long-term annualized return of the average mutual fund equity investor and the S&P 500 continued to decrease in 2012.
- The fixed-income investor experienced a return of 4.68 percent compared to an advance of 4.21 percent on the Barclays Aggregate Bond Index.
- The average fixed income investor has failed to keep up with inflation in nine out of the last 14 years.

It doesn't take a market research report to tell us that market volatility, or risk, is out of our control. That is a given. Without a sound investment plan and a proven system of investing, the average investor will usually underperform the market, sometimes by a wide margin. Because of limited resources, those same investors may find that their retirement goals and objectives will need to be altered as a result of their risk-taking. You must ask yourself, "Is taking more risk really worth it?"

## CHAPTER 8 RECAP //

- The deck is stacked against the ordinary investor. According to the DALBAR report, individual investors consistently underperform compared to the market because of a variety of factors, including emotional investing.

# 9
# THE LOVE OF LIQUIDITY

*The goal of retirement is to live off your assets, not on them.*
                                                    – Frank Eberhart

There are five key attributes to the saving of money: *Liquidity, Safety, Return, Risk and Taxes.* In a perfect world, the ideal investment would: be liquid (no withdrawal penalties), be safe (no risk) and earn a high rate of return free of tax. Such an investment would be the Holy Grail of the financial world if one could find it. Unfortunately, such an investment does not exist. The very nature of markets and investments leads to a diversity of investment choices, each with their own variations on these attributes.

In the real world, you can usually enjoy two or three of these attributes at the expense of the others. If safety and liquidity are the top priorities, then the rate of return would suffer. Such is the case with savings accounts. If safety and return are essential, then CDs or fixed annuities become viable options but only by forfeiting some liquidity. If liquidity and rate of return are important, then safety suffers, as is the case with stocks and other securities. Taxes are present in most investment options. A successful retirement plan will contain a proper balance of all of these attributes.

If there is one trait too many people are in love with, it is liquidity. The love of liquidity is a dangerous mistake that costs many people a more comfortable retirement and a greater legacy. This is one reason why so many investors love the stock market – it's liquid. They can sell or do something else with their money whenever their emotions dictate. On the flip side, the love of liquidity also keeps some people from ever committing their money to better earning investments such as the stock market. They won't consider any option for their money but bank accounts or the home safe. Sadly, I run into too many of these people and, as you can guess, they rarely do business with financial advisors.

So, if liquidity is important, is there a rule of thumb that can help determine how much of your portfolio should be liquid? Not really. The choice of liquidity is as personal as the choice of taking risk. The decision should be based on your particular goals and objectives. At the very least, however, I recommend the equivalent of six months of your monthly expenses to be maintained in a reserve fund, a point I addressed previously. The amount you would keep liquid above and beyond this minimum would depend on a number of factors. If your portfolio contains stocks and other securities that are already liquid, do these Yellow or Red monies have a stated purpose? If so, then you are accomplishing two goals: the growth you want and some needed liquidity.

You may want to ask yourself other questions regarding your liquidity needs. Are you expecting to replace the car soon? Are you planning to travel frequently? Is the house in need of repair or remodeling? Are you planning expensive medical procedures? Are there needy children or grandchildren who may require monetary assistance? These are just a few of the many reasons for maintaining adequate liquid funds.

The challenge is to limit your liquidity commitment to a realistic amount. Keeping too much money liquid just because it feels warm and fuzzy or because you won't trust an advisor for help can be a very costly decision. Savings accounts and CDs, for instance, do not provide enough return to stay ahead of inflation in most years. On the other hand, placing too much money in stocks or other securities subjects your money to unnecessary risk, unless these securities are earmarked for another purpose, such as providing growth in the portfolio.

## CASE STUDY

*Ted was a corn and soybean farmer with 1,200 acres of farmland. He was not a wealthy farmer. He just worked hard to provide a good living for himself and his family. He reinvested his profit from the farming operations into cattle and new crops for the coming year.*

*To sustain the liquid needs of his operation, Ted maintained somewhere between $60,000 and $80,000 in his checking and savings accounts throughout the year. He used this reserve fund to repair or replace equipment and to buy other needed supplies. When a need for additional cash arose, he couldn't harvest just one acre of soybeans and use them for payment. He needed some liquidity in order to remain a successful farmer.*

*When Ted finally retired his overalls and sold the farm, he placed the net gain from the sale directly into the bank where it still resides today. Ted keeps his profits in liquid, low-earning accounts because that's what Ted has always done. Old habits are hard to break. Ted has little understanding of money matters. He has no idea he is not even keeping up with inflation. His grown children have encouraged him to put the money to work but to no avail. Such things don't matter to Ted now that he's retired and the bank account is full of cash.*

Ted's case is a classic example of living "on" one's assets instead of "off" them. Hopefully, Ted and his wife won't experience a catastrophe or health issue or other emergency that would shrink the value of their life's work. Living too long is risk enough, since there are many years in which he withdraws more money than he earns at the bank, diminishing the principal. Utilizing The Rule of 100 and putting the money to work would most likely benefit Ted, his wife, children and grandchildren.

Many years ago I met with a prospective client who was interested in the higher earning power of an annuity. He was a licensed realtor but used the license mainly to buy and sell properties for himself. His net worth at the time was about $1.5 million. He maintained nearly half of that net worth in cash and CD's at the bank. This was money he would not risk in real estate. That was wise, in my opinion, and I complimented him on that decision. My attempts, however, to convince him to commit some of that cash to a much higher-earning, tax-deferred account backed by a life insurance company fell on deaf ears. His reasoning? Love of liquidity. He would not commit his money to a surrender charge period at any price. He would rather lose money to taxes and inflation than give up liquidity. Needless to say, he continued to lose money every year.

A word of advice: Don't fall in love with liquidity. It won't love you back.

## CHAPTER 9 RECAP //

- Liquidity is an essential element in a balanced retirement plan. Don't fall in love with it. It won't love you back. Use it sparingly or with a stated purpose, such as growth.

# 10
## TAXES AND RETIREMENT

*The only difference between death and taxes is that death doesn't get worse every time Congress meets.*

— Will Rogers

Taxes play a starring role in the theater of retirement planning. Everyone is familiar with taxes but not everyone is familiar with how to make tax planning a part of their retirement strategy.

Taxes are taxes, right? You'll pay them before retirement and you'll pay them during retirement. What's the difference? The truth is taxes are a **cost** of investing or saving. It's what you get to keep after the **cost** is deducted that matters. If there are investments that are taxed less than others, taxed at a later date, or not taxed at all, wouldn't you want to know about them? If taking income or withdrawals from one type of investment would **cost** you less in tax than another investment, wouldn't you rather take the income from the less-taxed option? Because of the complexity of the tax code, an open-minded approach to taxes can help you save money, protect your assets and ensure that your legacy remains intact.

Let's clarify before we begin that ***tax planning*** and ***tax reporting*** are two very different disciplines. Most people only *report* their taxes. March rolls around, they pull out a blank 1040 or use TurboTax to enter their income and taxable assets, and ship it off to the IRS so they can forget about it for another year. If you use a tax professional, you are essentially paying them to record history. You may feel better about your tax situation for a year but you're not addressing any root causes of **intaxication** (emotionally impaired because of high taxation).

Tax planning is the task of addressing and preventing intaxication before it starts. It involves being proactive with your taxes and planning ahead instead of falling a victim to history. I have told my clients for many years now that **taxes are the price you are paying for the financial decisions you've already made. Change those decisions and you'll change your tax picture.** Working with a financial professional who, along with a tax professional, makes recommendations about your finances will keep you looking forward instead of in the rearview mirror.

## TAXES AND RETIREMENT

When you retire, you move from the earning and accumulation phase of your life into the asset distribution phase of your life. For most people, that means relying on social security, a 401(k), an IRA or a pension. Most of these distributions will be considered income by the IRS and will be taxed as such. There are exceptions (not all of your social security income is taxed and income from Roth IRAs is not taxed), but for the most part, your distributions will be subject to income taxes.

If you own IRAs, for instance, when you reach 70 ½ years of age you will be required to withdraw a certain amount of money from them each year. The amount of the required withdrawal depends on your age and the year-end balance in your IRA. This amount is called a Required Minimum Distribution (RMD). Why are you required to withdraw money from these types of accounts? Because the government wants to collect the taxes on that growth. If you have a large balance in an IRA, there's a chance your RMD could increase your income significantly enough to put you into a higher tax bracket, subjecting you to a higher tax rate.

Here's where tax planning can pay off. In the distribution phase of your life, you have a predictable income based on your RMDs, your social security benefit and any other income-generating assets you may have. What really impacts you at this stage is how much of that distribution you get to keep after taxes. If you can reduce your overall tax burden by 10, 20 or even 30 percent, you earned more money that year because you were able to keep more money.

How do you save money on taxes? By changing the decisions you've already made. For instance, choosing tax-advantaged vehicles instead of taxable ones can help alleviate intaxication. A tax or financial professional can help you create a **distribution plan** that minimizes your taxes and maximizes your annual net income.

## BUILDING A TAX DIVERSIFIED PORTFOLIO

During the accumulation years when you were saving and investing, little thought may have been given to how distribution planning and tax planning will benefit your portfolio in the later years. Often, the more exciting prospect of investing and growing your assets ruled the day. Taxes, however, play a crucial role in retirement planning. Achieving tax efficiency requires knowledge of options, foresight and professional guidance.

Finding the path to a good tax plan isn't always a simple task. Every tax return you file is different from the one before it because things constantly change. Your expenses change. Planned or unplanned purchases occur. Health care costs, medical bills, an inheritance, property purchases, RMDs, travel, or any number of things can affect how much income you report and how many deductions, if any, you can take each year.

Preparing for the ever-changing landscape of your financial life requires a tax-diversified portfolio that can be leveraged to balance the incomes, expenditures and deductions that affect you each year. Ask yourself these questions:

- Do you have a tax-diversified portfolio that will meet your needs?
- Do you have a diversity of taxable and non-taxable income planned for your retirement?
- Will you be able to maximize your distributions to take advantage of your deductions when you retire?
- Is your portfolio tax-diversified enough to adapt to an ever-changing (and usually more exacting) tax code?

## CASE STUDY

*When Darlene returned home from the hospital after having heart surgery, the 77-year-old called her daughter, sister and brother to let them know she was home and feeling well. She should have also called her tax professional. Darlene's out-of-pocket medical expenses for the surgery, the part not covered by Medicare, amounted to more than $20,000.*

*Darlene could have deducted medical expenses in excess of 7.5 percent of Adjusted Gross Income (AGI). Her AGI was $40,000 that year, which would have allowed her to deduct most of those out-of-pocket medical expenses.* **Darlene, however, forgot to tell her tax professional about the surgery when she filled her taxes the**

***following year**. In addition, she is now past the three year period in which she can amend a prior tax return.*

This relatively simple example of how tax planning can save you money is just the tip of the iceberg. No one can be expected to know the entire U.S. tax code. It's so complicated that even those who make the tax laws hire tax specialists to interpret it for them. In like manner, an investor working with a team of tax and financial professionals has a huge advantage over the average taxpayer in interpreting the code to their benefit.

## PROACTIVE TAX PLANNING

The implications of proactive tax planning are far reaching, and are larger than many people realize. Remember, doing your taxes in February, March or April means you are writing a history book. Planning your taxes in October, November or December means that you are writing the story as it happens. You can look at all the factors that are at play and make decisions that will impact your tax return *before* you file it.

Realizing that tax planning is an element of financial planning is an important step to make. When you incorporate tax planning into your financial planning, it becomes part of the way you maximize your financial potential. Paying less in taxes means you keep more of your hard-earned money. Simply put, the more money you keep, the more of it you can leverage as an asset. For instance, if you are 40 years old, are you contributing the maximum amount to your 401(k) plan? Are you contributing to a Roth IRA? Do you have life insurance? Taxes affect all of these investment decisions.

There may be years in which you can benefit from higher distributions from your retirement assets because other tax issues caused your tax bracket to decline that year. There may be years when you have more itemized deductions than other years. **Cor-**

**relating your distributions with your available deductions is at the heart of smart tax planning.** Professional guidance can bring you to the next level of income distribution, allowing you to remain more tax efficient. Remember, saving money on taxes could earn you more money than changing the investments.

What you show on paper is important: your assets, savings and investments. It's just as important to know how to get it off paper and into your wallet. Almost anything that involves money also involves taxes. Annuities, IRAs, 401(k)s, 403(b)s, stocks, bonds and other investment options will have tax implications. Life itself has tax implications. Illness, surgeries, car repairs, *any event that has a financial impact on your life will likely have a corresponding tax implication.* Tax planning should be a part of these issues.

## CASE STUDY

*When Peter's father passed away, Peter became the beneficiary of his father's $500,000 IRA. Peter has a wife and four children, and he knew that his father had intended for a portion of the IRA to go toward funding the children's college educations. In addition, Peter had always had a dream of building a cabin up in the mountains as a summer retreat for the family. Now he had the money to build it.*

*After the estate was distributed, Peter, who is 50 years old and whose oldest son is entering college, decided to liquidate the IRA. By doing so, his taxable income for that year put him in a higher tax bracket subjecting him to 39.6 percent federal income tax and immediately reducing the value of the asset to $302,000. An additional 3.8 percent surtax on net investment income further diminished the funds to $283,000. Liquidating the IRA in effect subjected much of Peter's regular income to the surtax, as well. At this point, the IRA was taxed at 43.4 percent.*

*Peter's state taxes were an additional 9 percent. Fortunately for Peter and the other heirs, Dad's estate was just under the threshold* *that would have triggered an estate tax on top of all the other taxes. In the end, Peter's IRA inheritance was taxed at 52.4 percent, leaving him with only 47.6 percent of the original $500,000. While the after-tax inheritance paid for the education of his two sons, there will be little remaining to build a cabin. Poor tax planning robbed Peter of his longtime dream.*

As the above example shows, leaving an asset to your beneficiaries can be more complicated than it may seem. In the case of a traditional IRA, after federal, state and possibly estate taxes, the asset could literally diminish to as little as 25 percent of its original value.

Here's another example of how taxes have major implications on asset management:

## CASE STUDY

*Greg and Rhonda, both 62 years old, begin working with a financial professional in October. After restructuring their assets to reflect their risk tolerance and creating a retirement income using Green Money, they feel better about their retirement situation. They are planning to maximize their social security benefits when the time comes. They have also established a Yellow Money strategy with their investment professional.*

*When their professional asks them about their tax plan, Greg and Rhonda tell him that their CPA handles their taxes every year. Their professional asks, "I don't mean who does your taxes, I mean, who does your tax planning?" Greg and Rhonda aren't sure how to respond.*

*Their financial professional sends Greg and Rhonda's financial plan to the firm's tax professional. A tax projection was requested. A week later their professional calls them with a tax plan for the year that saved them more than $2,000 on their tax return. The couple was shocked. The firm's tax professional revealed that if they paid their* *estimated taxes before the end of the year, they would be able to itemize it as a deduction, allowing them to reduce their tax burden.*

This solution won't work for everyone, and it may not work for Greg and Rhonda every year. That's not the point. By being proactive with their approach to taxes and using the resources made available by their financial professional, they were able to create a tax plan that saved them money.

## YELLOW MONEY AND TAXES

There are also tax implications for the money that you have managed professionally. Accounts that are actively traded can particularly benefit from having a proactive tax strategy. Without going into too much detail, for tax purposes, there are two kinds of investment accounts: qualified and non-qualified. Qualified accounts such as IRAs, 401(k)s, etc., are usually taxed when withdrawn. The lone exception is Roth IRA accounts which are income tax-free.

In non-qualified accounts, different investment strategies can have different effects on how the gains are taxed. Some accounts benefit more from one kind of investment strategy than another. Determining how to plan for the taxation of non-qualified and qualified investments is fodder for holiday party discussions at accounting firms. While it may not be a stimulating topic for the average investor, you don't have to understand exactly how it works in order to benefit from it.

While there are many differences between qualified and non-qualified accounts, there is one main difference. Qualified plans are designed to give investors tax benefits by deferring taxation of their growth until they are withdrawn. Non-qualified investments are not eligible for these deferral benefits. An exception is an annuity, which is already tax-deferred. As such, non-qualified investment gains, dividends and/or interest are taxed each year whenever income is realized, whether it is withdrawn or not.

Actively and passively traded accounts provide a simple example of how to position your investments for the best tax advantage. In an actively managed portfolio, there is a high frequency of buying and selling of stocks, bonds, funds and ETFs in the hope of increasing the return. If that active portfolio does well and makes a 20 percent short-term gain one year and you are in the 39.6 percent tax bracket, your after-tax gain from that portfolio is about 12 percent (39.6 percent of 20 percent gain = 8 percent tax - the 20 percent gain = 12 percent gain after-tax). Using a qualified account such as an IRA, a 20 percent gain remains 20 percent because there is no tax on the gain that year. The gains are deferred until a later time when they will be taxed.

Does this mean that non-qualified accounts (taxable) should be passively traded rather than actively traded? Not necessarily. The question is, if you have qualified and non-qualified accounts, where do you want to position your actively managed and passively managed strategies? It's personal preference. But from a tax planning standpoint, keeping your actively managed investment strategies inside an IRA or some other qualified plan could allow you to realize the higher gains of those investments without paying tax on their growth every year. Your more passively managed strategies could then be used in taxable, non-qualified accounts. Less trading allows for longer holding periods on each asset purchased, thus subjecting those gains to more favorable long-term capital gain rates instead of ordinary income tax rates. This strategy also allows for more tax deferral in those accounts.

If you are interested in earning more on your investments, don't take more risk. Do better tax planning. To take advantage of tax strategies that maximize your net income, you need the strategies, experience and knowledge of a financial or tax professional.

At the end of the day, what's most important is not how much you earned, but how much you kept.

## ESTATE TAXES

The government doesn't just tax your investments while you're alive. They'll also dip into your legacy in the form of estate taxes after you're gone. In reality, it's a tax for being financially successful.

While estate taxes aren't a hot topic these days, they are still an issue of concern for the wealthy. Under the 2014 tax rules, the estate tax exemption is $5.34 million. This means if you are single and pass away in 2014 and you're accumulated wealth exceeds this exemption amount, estate taxes will be due. No federal estate taxes are due on estates less than $5.34 million. However, certain states have estate tax exemptions that are lower than the federal exemption. Some states are as low as $600,000. In other words, even though you may not be subject to federal taxation at death, you may still be subject to state taxation in some states.

There are a number of strategies for reducing the impact of estate taxes. By planning ahead, you can often preserve more of your legacy for the benefit of the heirs. One basic strategy used quite often is annual gifting. The 2014 annual gift tax exclusion is $14,000. You can gift up to this amount to as many different people as you would like each and every year. As I've always said, if you want to be remembered, gift money. Recipients of gifting can include children, their spouses, siblings, a friend you want to impress and even the author of this wonderful book. Reducing your taxable estate before you pass away reduces the amount of estate tax you will owe at death.

Another tax strategy to set up an irrevocable trust. The assets within the trust are exempt from estate taxes if set up and administered properly. Most often, gifts to the Trust are used to purchase a life insurance policy on the life of the grantor. Since life insurance policies typically pay income tax-free, this is a leveraged way to provide heirs with the money to pay estate taxes.

There are other estate planning strategies that can help reduce the impact of estate taxes. A financial or estate planning professional can help you choose the best strategies for your situation.

## CHAPTER 10 RECAP//

- Taxes are a cost of investing. Reduce the cost and you'll keep more of what you earn.
- Taxes are the price you're paying for the financial decisions you've made. Change those decisions and you can change your tax picture.
- Any event that has a financial impact on your life will likely have a corresponding tax implication.

# 11

## TAX-ADVANTAGED INVESTING

*I don't know if I can live on my income or not. The government won't let me try it.*

— Bob Thaves

Whether you are heading into retirement or are already retired, hopefully you have established **a diversified tax-advantaged plan.** The point to spending most of your life accumulating wealth is not to frame your net worth number on the wall next to the family pictures. The goal is to end up with as much money as possible in your pocket or the pocket of your loved ones. To truly understand tax diversification, you must understand what types of investments or accounts exist in this arena and how each of these will be treated during your accumulation and distribution years. We will discuss four types of money:

1. Free money
2. Tax-free money

3. Tax-deferred money
4. Tax deductible money

## FREE MONEY

Free money. Just the sound of these two words gives me the tingles. Who doesn't get excited about the prospect of free money? It's the best kind of money regardless of tax treatment because it is, well, free. Besides the obvious source of free money – gifts from relatives or friends – many employers offer free money to their employees in the form of matching 401(k) contributions or gifts of company stock. This is designed to encourage employee saving. With employer matching plans, the company will contribute up to a certain percentage of an employee's salary (generally 3 percent to 5 percent) toward that employee's retirement account when the employee contributes to their retirement account as well. For example, if an employee earns $50,000 annually and contributes 3 percent ($1,500) to their retirement account annually, the employer will also contribute 3 percent ($1,500) to the employee's account. That is $1,500 in free money. It will be taxed when withdrawn but it was still free.

If you're like most people, you won't be able to count on the free stuff to build your retirement plan. You'll have to earn it the hard way and find a way to save it the hard way. Those savings will then fall into one of the following tax classes.

## TAX-FREE MONEY

Tax-free or tax-exempt money generates interest or gains which will not be taxed when withdrawn. There are three types of tax-free instruments that we'll discuss: municipal bonds, Roth IRAs and life insurance.

**MUNICIPAL BONDS.** One of the most commonly known forms of tax-free or tax-exempt money is municipal bonds, which pay interest that could be tax-free on the federal level, state level or both. There are several caveats regarding tax-free income from municipal bonds that you should be aware of. States will generally tax the interest earned on a municipal bond unless that bond is offered from an entity located within that state. Second, municipal bond interest, even though it is federally tax-free, is added back into the equation for determining your modified adjusted gross income (MAGI) for social security taxation. If your MAGI is above a certain threshold, up to 85 percent of your social security is subject to taxation. In effect, if municipal bond interest subjects other income to taxation, then the municipal bond interest is not tax-free after all.

Lastly, municipal bond interest is included for determining tax under the alternative minimum tax (AMT) system. In its basic form, the AMT system is a separate tax system that applies if the tax computed under AMT exceeds the tax computed under the regular tax system. The difference between these two computations is the alternative minimum tax.

**ROTH IRAs.** Roth accounts are probably the single greatest tax tool to come from Congress in decades. Roth IRAs are well known but rarely used. They were first established by the Taxpayer Relief Act of 1997 and named after Senator William Roth, the chief sponsor of the legislation. Roth accounts are individual retirement accounts (IRAs) or employer sponsored retirement accounts that allow for tax-advantaged growth of earnings **and** tax-advantaged withdrawals.

The main difference between a traditional IRA and a Roth lies in the timing of the taxation. In an IRA or 401(k) plan, for instance, the contribution to the plan is not taxed in the year contributed. It is deducted from your taxable income. In addition, you will not pay tax on any earnings until withdrawn.

A Roth account, on the other hand, is funded with after-tax contributions. You pay the tax on the contribution at the moment it is contributed. Once inside the Roth, those monies grow income free of tax.

Another significant difference between an IRA and a Roth is how distributions are taxed in the later years. When you take a distribution from an IRA, the withdrawal is added to your ordinary income and taxed accordingly. Including this type of withdrawal in your income subjects it to the consequences mentioned above for taxation on social security , AMT, as well as higher Medicare premiums. Roth distributions, on the other hand, are income distributed without taxation and are not included in any calculations regarding social security, AMT, or Medicare taxes. To summarize, an IRA gives you the tax advantages up front but the Roth gives you the tax advantages on the back end.

So, why doesn't everyone utilize the advantages of a Roth? There are several reasons, but the single biggest reason has been the constraints on contributions. If you earned over certain thresholds (MAGI over $125,000 for those filing as single and $183,000 for those filing jointly for 2012), you were not eligible to make contributions to a Roth. Until recently, if your modified adjusted gross income (MAGI) was over $100,000 (single or joint), you could not convert a traditional IRA to a Roth. Today, there are no income restrictions to converting an IRA to a Roth. Outside these contribution limits, most people save for retirement through their employers and most employers do not offer Roth options in their plans. The reason behind this is because Roth accounts are not well understood and **people have been conditioned to take a deduction today and worry about the tax later rather than the other way around. However,** Roth IRAs are slowly gaining in popularity as people become more educated on the benefits.

**THE SUPER ROTH: LIFE INSURANCE.** As previously mentioned, Roth accounts and life insurance are the two best tax-advantaged tools to come out of Congress. Life insurance is greatly misunderstood as a tax tool, however. Most of us think of it as a necessary expense of living, not a tax tool. You may have purchased life insurance when you were younger to provide funds for your family and estate in case of your untimely death. You wanted to take care of the ones you loved, which is good purpose for owning life insurance. But now that you're approaching retirement or have already retired, you have probably thought: "I'll cut that expense from my budget. I have some wealth now and I don't need the expense anymore." This thinking is a direct result of not understanding the power of leveraging and tax planning.

Once you accumulate wealth, I agree that the **need** for life insurance dissipates. You probably don't need life insurance once you've amassed some wealth, the kids are out of the house, and the main worry is caring for a spouse. But here's the crux of the discussion: you don't **need** stocks, bonds, annuities or CDs either. They're financial tools that you've **chosen** for your portfolios. Nobody made you purchase them (hopefully). One of the most liberating feelings associated with getting older, becoming empty-nesters and accumulating some wealth is that you have more choices in how you live, what you do **and how you invest for the future.** Life insurance, for you, now becomes a choice – a tool – to help you achieve your goals and objectives, even though it may no longer be a need.

Life insurance is by far the best tax-advantaged device available. Better than a Roth? No, just different. Both plans pay tax-free benefits, which is a huge advantage over other investment vehicles. One difference, however, is "who" gets to benefit from the tax-free payout. A Roth is a plan **you** can utilize later in life. A life insurance policy is a plan that **someone you love** utilizes later in life. Unfortunately, the fact that someone else will enjoy the benefit instead of the insured keeps some people from even considering life insurance as a planning tool.

Another difference between life insurance and a Roth is how much you can contribute to the plan. The biggest advantage to life insurance is that the government has not placed restrictions on who can contribute or how much you can contribute to a policy. Anyone in reasonable health who can qualify with the insurance company can buy a policy in any amount they qualify for. Roth IRAs, however, are subject to the restrictions mentioned previously.

Why, then, do so few retirees own life insurance? The inability to qualify for a policy because of health issues keeps some seniors from using the benefits of life insurance in their retirement planning. This is why it's important to plan ahead while you're healthy. Misunderstanding is another reason for the lack of popularity among seniors. Many misunderstand that **life insurance is the only insurance you'll ever buy that is guaranteed to pay off.** It's not a gamble like most other insurances, if you buy the right type of policy. Some of us need to be reminded that **death is not a gamble, it's a certainty.**

## CASE STUDY

*At eighty years of age, Randy was healthy and wealthy. A retired dentist, Randy and his wife, Rebecca, had real estate holdings, stocks, CDs and an IRA totaling nearly $5 million.*

*Randy was an open-minded individual by nature. He was always willing to listen and learn from others. He scheduled time with a financial advisor to discuss his planning efforts. The advisor, after reviewing Randy's assets and goals, saw the need to address the estate tax implications of the portfolio. The advisor explained to Randy that if he and Rebecca died that year, only $2 million of their assets would pass free of estate tax to their children. The other $3 million would be taxed.*

Randy and his advisor agreed on two things. First, because Rebecca was struggling with health issues, Randy would most likely survive her. Second, because real estate was the major holding in their portfolio, it is a non-liquid asset. Estate taxes are due within nine months after the second death and this creates a liquidity problem in their portfolio.

To help solve the liquidity issue, the advisor recommended that Randy leverage his IRA money by applying for a $1 million universal life insurance policy. The annual premium of $53,000 would mostly come from the required minimum distributions that were already being paid from the IRA, which had a balance of $759,735 that year. Leveraging the IRA in this way would help cover potential estate taxes.

Randy's health allowed him to qualify for the $1 million life policy. All went as planned for the next five and a half years. Suddenly, Randy passed away in his sleep at the age of 86, much to the surprise of everyone.

The total premium paid into the life insurance policy was $265,000 at the date of death. The value of the IRA at that time was $690,567. Rebecca inherited the IRA and received a tax-free $1 million check from the life insurance company.

Using the leveraging power of life insurance, an asset worth $759,735 was leveraged into $1.69 million in five and a half years with 59 percent of it qualifying as tax-free income.

There are two main types of life insurance policies: term and permanent. The best way to remember the differences is to compare them to a home. You can rent a home or buy a home. If you rent a home, the rent payments will be less expensive than a mortgage, but you'll build no equity and you live at the mercy of the landlord who can choose to increase your rent or not renew your lease when it expires. This is how term insurance works.

If you can afford to buy a home instead, you know you'll pay more in monthly payments, but you'll build equity and nobody can ever evict you unless you stop making the payments. You can die there if you choose and pass the home on to your spouse or heirs. This is how permanent insurance works. Once you obtain it, you own it for life.

Term life insurance policies are best utilized when you need to cover the risk of death for only a specific period of time. Term policies can be level premium for a stated number of years, such as 10 or 20 years, or they can be increasing premium that covers you as long as you continue paying the premiums.

Permanent polices, such as whole life or universal life, have an equity feature called cash value. When you make a premium payment on the policy, part of the payment pays the cost of insurance and the balance goes into the cash value account and earns interest. Building up the cash value in the early years is what helps pay the rising cost of insurance as you age. This is why most permanent policies can have a level premium for life.

If the cash value is large enough, you can actually take tax-free withdrawals during retirement to supplement your income. This is another tax-advantaged benefit of life insurance. As long as there is cash value to pay the costs of insurance, the death benefit can remain intact, although it will be reduced by the withdrawals.

Now that we've identified the differences between policies, I have a question for you longtime owners of term insurance: If you know it makes more sense to buy a home than rent one, why are you renting your life insurance instead of buying it? Is a house more important to you than your life?

Making the right life insurance decision can bring valuable tax advantages to your planning.

## TAX-DEFERRED MONEY

Tax-deferred money is the type of money most people are familiar with. IRAs, annuities and employer sponsored retirement plans such as 401(k), 403(b) and 457 plans are prime examples of tax-deferred money. Once you fund one of these types of accounts, the earnings grow tax-deferred until withdrawn.

Think of tax-deferred instruments as a cup. The cup is a utensil to hold water, coffee, juice or whatever you decide to pour into it. As long as nothing spills out, the cup has fulfilled its purpose. Tax-deferred instruments are cups that hold whatever you decide to pour into them – stocks, bonds, annuities, CDs, etc. The cup protects the contents from spilling out, or in other words, from being taxed. You pay tax on the contents only when they leave the cup.

You would utilize tax-deferred accounts when you expect your tax rate to be lower upon withdrawal of the funds. You're essentially kicking the can down the road. Taxes will be due at some point but you enjoy some tax relief each year you are deferring the earnings. In addition, the taxes you would have paid on the gains remain in the account where they continue to earn. This compounding of gains can be very beneficial over time. The longer you defer paying the tax, the greater the compounding value of not paying the tax. Once withdrawals begin, however, the gains will not only be taxed but the withdrawals could trigger other negative tax consequences such as tax on social security, as previously discussed.

## TAX DEDUCTIBLE MONEY

Many types of tax-deferred accounts are also tax deductible, meaning you do not pay tax on the contributions. As long as you live the rules the government has stipulated for these plans, you qualify to deduct the contributions. Tax-deductible plans are referred to as qualified plans. Employer sponsored plans and IRAs are examples of qualified plans.

They enjoy both the benefits of tax deductibility and tax deferral.

Qualified plans are subject to withdrawal rules that do not apply to non-qualified plans. These rules require withdrawals to begin no later than the year in which the owner turns age 70 ½. The amount of the withdrawal is also stipulated by regulation and increases as you age. Because you have not paid tax on the original contributions or the gains yet, withdrawals from qualified plans are fully taxed as ordinary income.

## TAX-EQUIVALENT YIELD

Any discussion of taxation of investments should include an understanding of tax-equivalent yield. This is the measuring stick to help you determine if a taxable bond, for instance, has a better yield for you than a tax-free bond, given similar bond risks. To determine the tax-equivalent yield, you divide the tax-free yield by 1 minus your tax bracket.

$$\text{Tax-equivalent yield} = \frac{\text{Tax-Free Yield}}{1 - \text{Tax rate}}$$

If you consider a tax-free bond that yields 5 percent and you're in the 25 percent tax bracket then any taxable bond yielding 6.66 percent or more would pay you more interest.

## CASE STUDY

*Bob and Mary are currently retired. Their income consists of social security, a small pension and investment interest. They're in the 25 percent tax bracket. They have a substantial portion of their investments in municipal bonds yielding 6 percent. The tax equivalent yield they would need to earn from a taxable investment would be 8 percent. Given the current interest rate environment and market volatility, Bob and Mary are not comfortable taking the risk that would be required to obtain taxable bonds earning more than 8 percent interest.*

*However, Bob & Mary discovered that the interest from their municipal bonds is not exempt from the social security tax calculation. In other words, 85 percent of their social security is being taxed because of the municipal bond interest. This reduces the after-tax yield on the bonds to 4.725 percent and the tax-equivalent yield to 6.3 percent. Bob & Mary are now considering some taxable bonds in the portfolio as long as the tax-equivalent yield on those bonds exceeds 6.3 percent.*

Regardless of the tax-advantaged choice you make today on your investments, you can count on the government changing the rules down the road for reasons discussed below. This is why regular tax analysis and adjustments are needed in any retirement plan to be successful. Utilizing a tax diversified approach in your planning can leave you with more money to accomplish your dreams and goals.

## THE FUTURE OF TAXATION

Tax legislation over the course of American history has delivered one resounding message: taxes go up, seldom down. We hear this message so often that it sounds like the boy who cried wolf: we don't bother caring anymore. The reason for the indifference about tax increases is because tax hikes usually do not take effect until two or three years after their introduction. The subsequent implementation of the changes occurs in steps, so it doesn't seem as painful. The politicians hope that time will cool the public outrage. The result can be equated to death by a thousand paper cuts.

## DEBT CEILING – CAUSE AND EFFECTS

The raising of the debt ceiling recently raises more than just the ability for our government to go further into debt. It also raises concerns and fears about the future of our economy. We are now seeing wider swings in the investment markets caused by uncertainty surrounding the economy. Recent discussions on raising the debt ceiling were coupled with discussions on major tax reforms needed to correct some of the problems underlining the government's free-spending ways.

Increasing the debt ceiling was needed because the government maxed out its credit card, so to speak, which it has been using for some time now. This coincides with the increasing use of credit by Americans, too. Unfortunately, most of us do not have the ability to get a credit limit increase on our credit cards once we reach the maximum limit, unless we can show the ability to pay back the balance. The only way you and I can pay back our cards is by spending less or earning more money. The government, however, is above this law of finance.

Now that the debt ceiling is raised, again, the government has been given a higher credit limit but it still hasn't come to grips with its spending habits or its revenue stream. The only way the government takes in revenue is by collecting taxes. Unfortunately, at the current moment, the government is collecting approximately $120 billion less per month than it currently spends so it has to borrow more money to survive.

## DEBT AND EARNINGS

Let us take a closer look at where we are today. The U.S. national debt is increasing at an alarming rate, rising to levels never seen before and threatening serious harm to the economy. As of the beginning of 2011, the national debt had risen to $13.6 trillion, averaging an 11.4 percent increase annually over the previous five years and a 9.2 percent increase annually over the previous 10 years. To put this into perspective, the national gross domestic product (GDP) has increased to $14.5 trillion during the same period, averaging a 2.9 percent annual increase over the previous five years and a 3.9 percent increase over 10 years. At the beginning of 2011, the national debt level was 93 percent of GDP. Economists believe that a sustainable economy exists at a maximum level of approximately 80 percent. As of December 20, 2013, the U.S. national debt was 107.69 percent of GDP with the debt at $17.25 trillion and the GDP at $16.02 trillion.*

The significance of these two numbers lies within the contrast. The national debt is the amount that needs to be repaid. This is the credit card balance. Gross domestic product, on the other hand, is less known and represents the market value of all goods and services produced within a country during a given period. Essentially, GDP represents the gross taxable income available to the government. If debts are increasing at a greater rate than the gross income available for taxation, then the only way to make up the difference is by increasing the rate at which the gross income is taxed.

The most recent presidential budget shows a continuing trend in the disparity between growth in the national debt and GDP over the next two decades. Although the increasing disparity is a real concern and shows that, at least in the short run, the federal deficit will not be addressed to counteract the potential crisis ahead, it is the revenue collection that tells the disconcerting story. Over the past 40 years, the average collection of GDP has been approximately 17.6 percent and currently collections are at approximately 14.4 percent of GDP.

As the presidential budget reveals, the projected revenues are estimated to be 20 percent by the end of the next decade. That is a 38.8 percent increase from the current tax levels. To put this

---

*http://www.usdebtclock.org/ 12/20/13

into perspective, if you are currently in the top tax bracket of 35 percent and this bracket increases by the proposed collection increase, your tax rate will be approximately 48.5 percent. Keep in mind that even at this rate the deficit is projected to increase.

## 2013 – THE END OF AN ERA?

From a historical point of view, taxes are low. The last time the U.S. national debt was at the same percentage level of GDP as today was at the end of World War II and several years following. The maximum tax rate averaged 90 percent from 1944 through 1963. Compare that to the maximum rate of 35 percent today and it becomes very clear that there is a disparity of extreme proportions.

Taxes during this historical period were at extreme levels for nearly 20 years. A significant point to note about the difference between that time period and today is the economic activity. Today, we are mired in extreme volatility with frequent periods of boom and bust at the same time we are witnessing the beginning of the greatest retirement wave ever experienced in U.S. history.

To contrast these two time periods with respect to the recovery period is almost impossible, since the external pressures from globalization and domestic unfunded liabilities did not exist or were irrelevant factors during the prior period.

To add insult to injury, U.S. domestic unfunded liabilities are currently estimated somewhere around $61.6 trillion due to Social Security, Medicare and government pensions, according to www.usdebtclock.org. The most troubling part of this dilemma pertains to the coming wave of Boomer retirees who will begin drawing their unfunded Social Security and Medicare entitlements. Over the long-run, expenditures related to Medicare and Medicaid are projected to grow faster than the economy overall.

To put the unfunded liabilities into perspective, consider them as "off-balance-sheet obligations," similar to those of Enron.

Although these are not listed as part of the national debt, they must be paid. These liabilities exist outside of the annual budgetary debt discussed. The difference between Enron and the U.S. unfunded liabilities is that if the U.S. government cannot generate the revenue from taxation to pay these liabilities, they will just print even more money and we'll go deeper into debt.

## THE SOLUTION?

Printing money as a way out of our debt problems is funny math. This creates inflationary pressures that devalue the U.S. dollar and make everyone less wealthy. Cutting the entitlements that compose this liability leaves millions of people without benefits they have come to expect. The only other option, and one that the government knows all too well, is increasing taxes. In fact, according to a Congressional Budget Office paper issued in 2004:

"The term 'unfunded liability' has been used to refer to a gap between the government's projected financial commitment under a particular program and the revenues that are expected to be available to fund that commitment. But no government obligation can be truly considered 'unfunded' because of the U.S. government's sovereign power to tax – which is the ultimate resource to meet its obligations."

A balanced budget will be required at some point and with this will come higher taxes. At that time, the Bush-era tax cut extensions put in place in December 2010 will have expired. Tax increases are inevitable, at this point. Whether those increases affect only the top income earners or unilaterally across all income levels is yet to be seen, but an increase of some sort will most certainly occur.

When should you start preparing for increased taxation? Now is the time to prepare. Structure countermeasures for the good, the bad and the ugly of each of these legislative nightmares by utilizing tax-advantaged retirement planning.

**You can often earn more money by reducing your taxes than by changing your investments.** In other words, it takes $1.40 in earnings to end up with a dollar after paying the tax. If you reduce your taxes on other earnings by a dollar, you now have $2 in your pocket.

As simple as it sounds, I agree that it is difficult to execute. Most people fail to put together a plan as they near retirement. That plan should begin with a simple cash flow budget. If you have not analyzed your proposed income streams and expenses, you will not be able to structure an efficient tax plan.

We spend our whole lives saving and accumulating wealth but spend so little time determining how to distribute this accumulation effectively. You need to make sure you have the appropriate diversification of taxable versus non-taxable assets to complement your distribution strategy.

## CHAPTER 11 RECAP //

- Tax diversification is another important tool in successful money management.
- When it comes to taxation, there are four types of money: free money, tax-free money, tax deferred money, and tax deductible money.
- You can count on government changing the tax rules in the future so analyze your tax situation regularly and make adjustments as needed.

# 12

# IRA TO ROTH: CONVERT OR NOT CONVERT?

*Money often costs too much.*

– Ralph Waldo Emerson

Louis Brandeis provides one of the best examples of how tax planning works. Brandeis was Associate Justice of the Supreme Court of the United States from 1916 to 1939. Born in Louisville, Kentucky, Brandeis was an intelligent man with a touch of country charm. He described tax planning this way:

"I live in Alexandria, Virginia. Near the Court Chambers, there is a toll bridge across the Potomac. When in a rush, I pay the dollar toll and get home early. However, I usually drive outside the downtown section of the city and cross the Potomac on a free bridge.

The bridge was placed outside the downtown Washington, D.C. area to serve a useful social service – getting drivers to drive the extra mile and help alleviate congestion during the rush hour.

If I went over the toll bridge and through the barrier without paying a toll, I would be committing tax evasion.

If I drive the extra mile and drive outside the city of Washington to the free bridge, I am using a legitimate, logical and suitable method of tax avoidance, and I am performing a useful social service by doing so."

The tragedy is that *few people know that the free bridge exists.* Like Brandeis, most American taxpayers have options when it comes to "crossing the Potomac," so to speak. It's a tax or financial planner's job to tell you what options are available. You can wait until March to file your taxes, at which time you might pay someone to report and pay the government a larger portion of your income. However, you could work with your financial or tax professional and incorporate a tax plan as part of your overall financial planning strategy before the year ends.. Filing a return after the year ends is like crossing the toll bridge. Tax planning before the year ends is like crossing the free bridge. Which makes more sense?

Most people want to save money and pay less in taxes. What makes this desire difficult in the real world is two things. First, we're in a hurry and want to take the quickest road home regardless of the cost. Second, the signs along the road directing us to the free bridge are often obscured and can't be read. Even if they could be read, what on earth did they mean anyway? Trying to read the tax code is like picking a scab off your arm. It's less painful to just ignore it. All we really want to know is: What are our options and the cost in taxes accompanying those options?

## ROTH IRA CONVERSIONS

The attractive qualities of Roth IRAs may have prompted you to explore the possibility of moving some of your assets into a Roth account. There are valuable advantages to doing a conversion but there are some challenges you'll want to be aware of before you convert.

There are a lot of reasons to look at a Roth conversion. One reason is to eliminate the Required Minimum Distributions (RMD). When you turn 70 ½ years old, you are required to take a minimum amount of money out of a traditional IRA. This amount is your RMD. It is treated as taxable income. As an example, a 71 year old IRA owner with a $500,000 balance will have an RMD of $18,867 that will be added to taxable income that year, whether it is wanted or not. The government wants the tax. And now! Deferring the tax is no longer allowed. Increasing your taxable income because of an RMD may not only increase your tax rate, it may also increase the tax you pay on your social security that year. That's quite a gift to Uncle Sam, isn't it? And he won't even give you a kiss or send a thank you card.

Why, then, would you convert to a Roth? Because **Roth IRAs do not have RMDs and their distributions are not taxable.** You can grow the Roth free of tax for decades and take advantage of a truly tax-free instrument. You will never pay tax on it again and neither will your beneficiaries. It is a valuable income tool and a valuable wealth transfer tool.

The biggest challenge of a Roth conversion is the tax you will pay on the amount of the conversion. Since your IRA has not been taxed yet, you must pay the tax on it before converting to a forever tax-free Roth account. This alone keeps many would-be converters from doing a conversion. Depending on your tax bracket and the amount of the conversion, the tax could be sizable and may not make sense for some taxpayers.

If you can afford to pay the tax, the earlier you convert to a Roth the better. Time is your ally. The longer the Roth account can grow tax-free, the bigger the after-tax benefit. It often makes sense to convert to a Roth before you retire and file for social security. Remember, if your income gets too high, your social security will be taxed. Regardless, it may still make sense to tax your social security one year in order to obtain the benefits of a Roth. Tax-free retirement income will become more valuable as the government raises tax rates in the future, which, as I wrote about earlier, is very likely. If you don't utilize the account later on, it becomes a valuable tax-free gift to someone you love. They'll always remember you for it. As I've often said, "**Never forget that the size of your funeral will always depend upon the weather… and the expected inheritances.**"

Your financial or tax professional will likely tell you that it is not a matter of whether or not you should perform a Roth conversion, it is a matter of how much and when.

Here are some things to consider before converting to a Roth IRA:

- If you convert before you retire, you may end up paying higher taxes on the conversion because you may already be in a high tax bracket because of your earnings. Sometimes it is better to wait until the year after you retire when you're taxable income and tax bracket have dropped.

- Some people opt to reduce their work hours from full-time to part-time in the years preceding retirement. This would be an opportune time to consider a Roth conversion.

- You could consider a Roth conversion in a year in which you have significant tax deductions. Here are some potential options:

- *Using medical expenses that exceed 10 percent of your Adjusted Gross Income (7.5 percent if you are age 65 or older). If you have sizable health care costs that you can list as* itemized deductions, you can convert an amount of income from an IRA to a Roth IRA that is offset by the deductible amount.

- *Individuals, usually small business owners, who are dealing with a Net Operating Loss (NOL).* If you have NOLs, but aren't able to utilize all of them on your tax return, you can carry them forward to help offset the taxable income from a Roth conversion.
- *Charitable giving.* If you are charitably inclined, you can use the amount of your donations to reduce your taxable income. By matching the amount you convert to a Roth to the amount of your charitable gift, you can essentially avoid taxation on the conversion. You may want to double your donations to a charity in one year, giving them two years' worth of donations in order to offset a Roth conversion.
- *Investments that are subject to depletion.* Certain qualified investments can kick off depletion expenses which can be used to offset a conversion.

There are many other options for offsetting conversion taxes, and a tax or financial professional can help you find and understand your options.

If you have a traditional IRA, Roth conversions are something to seriously consider.

## THE VALUE OF TAX DIVERSIFICATION

Is it better to have a Roth IRA or traditional IRA? It depends. Some people don't mind having taxable income from an IRA. Their taxable income might be low and the resulting RMDs might not affect their tax bracket to any substantial degree. If they're in a position where little of their social security benefit is subject to tax and their RMD is small, then an IRA is not a tax burden to them.

There are situations where you can leverage taxable income to your advantage.

## CASE STUDY

*Darrel and Linda have dreamt of buying a boat when they retire. It is something they have looked forward to their entire marriage. In addition to their IRA and other investments for retirement, they have set aside some money for the sole purpose of purchasing a boat.*

*When the time arrives, Darrel and Linda purchase the boat of their dreams. They pay $15,000 in sales tax on the boat purchase, which is a deductible expense on the tax return. Their financial professional advises them to convert $15,000 of an IRA to a Roth to offset the tax deduction. In the end, they pay zero tax on their Roth conversion.*

The moral of the story? ***Having a tax diversified portfolio gives you options***. Having a combination of tax-advantaged sources in your portfolio can offer opportunities to maximize your tax benefits. Remember, it's not what you accumulate that matters, it's what you keep.

## CHAPTER 12 RECAP //

- Look for the "free bridge" option in your tax planning. Converting from an IRA to a Roth is taking the free bridge in retirement.
- Converting to a Roth can also help you preserve and build your legacy.
- Having a tax diversified portfolio gives you options that may provide valuable benefits later on.

# 13
## PREPARING YOUR LEGACY

*I don't feel old. I don't feel anything until noon. Then it's time for my nap.*

*— Bob Hope*

If you're like most people, planning your estate isn't on the top of your list of things to do on a Sunday afternoon. Planning your retirement, managing your assets and just living your life are more likely to take precedence over how your assets will pass after death. The sad truth is that if you don't plan your legacy, someone else will. That someone will be a group of complete strangers who care little about your particular wishes. Those strangers will consist of judges, court clerks and attorneys. Who do you think has the best interests of your beneficiaries in mind?

There is more to planning a legacy than just maximizing your estate. When some people think about an estate, they think of a stately southern mansion filled with grinning servants whistling

*Dixie.* But an estate is not just something the wealthy possess. An estate is part of your legacy and that legacy is more than the sum total of the financial assets you've accumulated. Your legacy is the lasting impression you make on those you leave behind. Dollars and cents are just one measuring rod of who you are and what you've accomplished.

A legacy encompasses your assets, achievements, stories and values. An estate may pay for the college tuition of a grandchild, but a legacy would instill in those grandchildren the importance of higher education, self-reliance and achievement. A legacy may also contain items of emotional significance such as family heirlooms, a piece of artwork you painted, a wood carving, a poem you wrote, family photos, your diaries, even your genealogy, anything that represents you or tells who you are.

Most people don't begin planning their legacy until some triggering event such as a heart attack or the death of a loved one. The emotional stress of these situations can make it more difficult to make patient, thoughtful decisions. Taking the time to premeditate and plan your legacy will assure that your assets and your memories will transfer according to your wishes and desires.

## THE BENEFITS OF PLANNING YOUR LEGACY
The distribution of your assets, whether in the form of real estate, stocks, bonds, IRAs, 401(k)s or cash, can be a complicated undertaking if you haven't left clear instructions for their distribution. Not having a plan will often cost money and time, leaving your loved ones waiting for years to receive what could have transferred in a matter of days. Instead of leaving transfer decisions to family members, attorneys, or financial professionals, help preserve your legacy and wishes by drafting a clear plan at an early age.

Taking the time to plan ahead can have some immediate benefits too. It can remind you how short life really is, which can offer a new perspective on your remaining years. Planning also allows time for a thoughtful assessment of your many blessings. Gratitude is the best cure for many of the ills that vex us, especially the ones in retirement.

Of course, knowing what we ought to do and doing it are two different activities. It requires time and effort to plan ahead and it may seem like a daunting task but the rewards can be priceless. As the Nike commercial says, **"Just Do It!"** One thing's for sure, *if you don't do it, it will be impossible for your assets, your memories, and your wishes to be transferred according to your desires.*

To begin the process, here are a few of the questions you might want to ask yourself:

- Have my primary and contingent beneficiaries been clearly designated?
- Does my plan allow for restriction of a beneficiary?
- Does my legacy plan address minor children that I want to provide for?
- Does my legacy plan allow for multi-generational payout?

## CASE STUDY

*The Friedmans were happily married for nearly twenty years when Anne, a former city school principal, died suddenly of a massive heart attack in September 2001.*

*Friedman said he never doubted he'd be entitled to the lump sum payment of $900,862 because the Teacher's Retirement System sent out annual statements that indicated his wife had named no beneficiary.*

*But after she died, officials found a form which had been filled out 27 years ago, four years before the couple met on a blind date in 1978.*

*It indicated Anne's mother, uncle and sister should inherit the money.*

*Anne's mother and uncle died, so the money was awarded to her sister, Virginia McLaughlin, and Friedman claims that she won't give him a cent.*

*"I think Anne would just be shocked," said Friedman, adding that he's just making ends meet. "[Virginia] won't sit down with me or my attorney. I'm just baffled." McLaughlin declined to comment.*

*A Manhattan Supreme Court ruling held that Anne's intention of making her husband the beneficiary could not be assumed and that the paperwork on file was clear, said Joseph Harbeson of the Corporation Council's office, which is representing the retirement system.*

*"We feel we're complying with the law as it stands."*

*The Supreme Court decision was upheld by the Appellate Division in December.*

*Friedman's lawyer, Sanford Young, described last month's decision as "sobering," and had some advice for all couples: Make sure you update your pension beneficiary forms. If you don't, your spouse and family may wind up with nothing.*

*New York Post, 1/31/ 2005*

**Start with a List.** The first step to preparing a legacy that reflects your desires is creating a detailed inventory of your assets and debts (if you have any). You need to know what assets you have, who the beneficiaries are, how much they are worth and how they are titled. More importantly, your heirs need to know this information. A list they can find is an immense help to grieving loved ones who are trying to wrap up your affairs. The list will also be essential for a financial or legal professional to be able to offer assistance in your planning.

Once you've itemized your assets, it's important to know how these assets will transfer to others. The most common methods for transferring assets are a will, trusts or beneficiary designations. Assets that transfer per a trust or by beneficiary designation avoid the probate process. A will, however, is subject to probate, which makes it a less effective transfer tool.

## CASE STUDY

*Jack started planning his retirement many years before he retired. He separated his **I Hope So** Money from his **I Know So** Money by using The Rule of 100. He turned most of his Red Money to Yellow Money by hiring an investment advisor to manage that money. He had a plan to maximize his social security and much of his Green Money was invested in indexed annuities to fill the income gap after retirement. He also converted some of his IRA to a Roth in a year in which his income decreased because of a job loss. But there was still something missing from his planning.*

*Jack decided to visit an estate attorney to update his will. He had not followed the advice of his investment advisor to establish a trust. After meeting with the attorney, Jack learned that his impressive attention to detail regarding the investment accounts had not carried over into his legacy planning. The attorney made it clear how Jack had jeopardized the distribution of his assets when he passes away. The two main problems with Jack's current estate plan were **probate** and **unintentional disinheritance**.*

## PROBATE

Probate's ugly reputation is well deserved. It can be a costly, time consuming process that diminishes your estate and can delay the distribution of your estate to your loved ones. Unless you've made a clear legacy plan and discussed options for avoiding probate, it is highly likely some if not most of your assets will pass through probate. ***If your will and beneficiary designations aren't correctly structured, some of these assets will go through the probate process, which can turn dollars into cents.***

Probate proceedings are notoriously expensive, lengthy and ponderous. A typical probate process identifies all of your assets and debts, pays any taxes and fees that you owe (including estate tax), pays court fees, attorney's fees, and then distributes your property and assets to your designated heirs. This process can take a few months or even years to finalize.

Probate is a public process. Because it happens in court, the assets that are probated become part of the public record. While this may not seem like a big deal to some people, others don't want that kind of intimate information available to the public.

Additionally, if much of your estate is distributed via your will, money needed by the family to cover the costs of your medical bills, funeral expenses and estate taxes will be tied up in probate. While immediate family members may have the option of requesting immediate cash from your assets during probate to cover these expenses, that process comes with its own set of complications. Choosing alternative methods for distributing your legacy can make life easier for your loved ones and can help them claim more of your estate in a more timely fashion.

## UNINTENTIONALLY DISINHERITING YOUR FAMILY

You would never want to unintentionally disinherit a loved one because of confusion surrounding your legacy plan. Unfortunately, it happens. Mistakes regarding legacy distribution usually hit the people you care about the most in your later years: the grandchildren.

One of the most important ways to plan an inheritance for your grandchildren is by properly structuring the distribution of your legacy, specifically, by choosing *per stirpes* over *per capita* designations.

**Per Stirpes.** *Per stirpes* is a legal term in Latin that means "by the branch." Your estate will be distributed *per stirpes* if you designate each branch of your family to receive an equal share of your estate. In the event that your children predecease you, their share will be distributed evenly between their children, your grandchildren.

**Per Capita.** *Per capita* distribution is different in that you may designate different amounts of your estate to be distributed to members of the same generation.

Per stirpes distribution of assets will follow the family tree down the line as the predecessor beneficiaries pass away. On the other hand, per capita distribution of assets ends on the branch of the family tree with the death of a designated beneficiary. For example, when your child passes away, in a per capita distribution, your grandchildren would not receive distributions from the assets that you designated to your child.

## CASE STUDY
*Jack decided to establish a living trust to avoid the costly and time-consuming hassle of probate. Some of his assets already enjoy probate-free status: his IRA, Roth and annuity. The living trust helped complete his legacy plan by converting his probated assets to trust assets. The trust made it possible for his assets to transfer exactly as he designated while keeping his financial affairs private and off the public record.*

Jack also learned of the value of utilizing two other financial tools to supercharge his legacy planning efforts: a stretch IRA and life insurance.

## STRETCH IRA: A LEGACY OF DOLLARS AND SENSE
In 1986, the U.S. Congress passed a law that allowed for multi-generational distributions of IRA assets. This method of distribution is called stretching your IRA or "stretch IRA" for short. This method stretches the distribution of the account over a long period of time to several beneficiaries. It also allows the account to continue accumulating value over that time period. You can use a stretch IRA as a planning tool that distributes income throughout

your lifetime, your children's lifetimes and even your grandchildren's lifetimes. Stretch IRAs are an attractive option for those who wish to create income for their loved ones rather than leave them a lump sum that may be subject to a high tax rate.

Under traditional IRA distribution rules, non-spousal beneficiaries must generally take distributions from their inherited IRAs, whether transferred or not, within five years after the death of the IRA owner. An exception to this rule applies if the beneficiary elects to take distributions over his or her lifetime, which is referred to as stretching the IRA. Below is an example of the power of stretching an IRA.

## Advantages of Stretching Your IRA

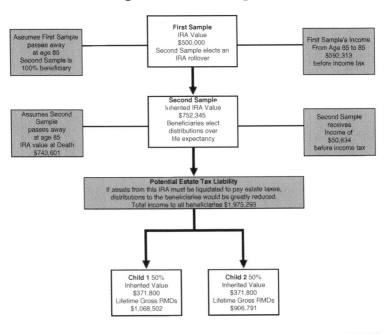

*This illustration represents a hypothetical situation and is for informational purposes only.*

## Personalized Data Sheet

|  | First Sample Cient | Second Sample Client |  |
|---|---|---|---|
| **Gender** | Male | Female |  |
| **Date of Birth** | January 01, 1949 | January 01, 1950 |  |
| **Age** | 65 | 64 |  |
| **Assumed Age at Death** | 85 | 85 |  |
| **Age at First Sample's Death** |  | 84 |  |
| **Current Value of IRA** | $500,000 |  |  |
| **Assumed Rate of Return** | 6.00% |  |  |
| **Owner/Spouse Tax Rate** | 20% |  |  |
| **Beneficiary Tax Rate** | 20% |  |  |
| **Heir** | **Age** | **Age at Second Sample's Death** | **Inheritance** |
| Child 1 | 30 | 52 | 50.00% |
| Child 2 | 35 | 57 | 50.00% |

When an IRA is distributed at the death of the owner, it can be tempting for a beneficiary to take a lump sum of money rather than stretching the IRA, regardless of the cost of taxation. If you are concerned about spendthrift beneficiaries, you can incorporate a "spendthrift" clause in the beneficiary designation to address this issue. A spendthrift clause will ensure your legacy is stretched appropriately and to your specifications. Only certain insurance companies allow this option.

## LIFE INSURANCE

Life insurance is a highly efficient legacy planning tool because it creates money when it is needed or desired the most. This Green Money asset can provide many benefits to get the most out of your legacy. Some of them include:

- Providing beneficiaries with a tax-free, liquid asset.
- Covering estate taxes or other costs associated with your death.
- Providing income for your dependents.

- Offering an investment opportunity for your beneficiaries.
- Covering expenses such as tuition or mortgage down payments for your children or grandchildren.
- Adding an option to include long-term care (LTC) or chronic illness benefits should you require them.

Very few people want life insurance and, as I discussed in a previous chapter, very few people will actually need it after retirement. But everyone wants what life insurance provides. They just don't want to pay for it or they can't qualify to get it. What life insurance provides is a tax-free sum of money for someone you love. You simply make small annual payments until your death. You can also deposit a one-time lump sum to pay up the policy. Either way, life insurance is specifically and uniquely capable of creating money when it is needed most.

It has been said that when you have money, you have options. When you don't have money, your options are limited. A life insurance policy can give your family and loved ones options that would otherwise be impossible to provide from other assets.

## CASE STUDY

*Ben spent the last twenty-five years building a small business. Each of his three children, Maddie, Ruby and Edward, worked in the shop part-time during high school. After all three attended college, only Maddie returned and joined her father in the business. Rudy married and now her family is her career. Edward pursued a career in electrical engineering.*

*Ben is able to retire comfortably on social security and income from the business but the business is basically his entire financial legacy. Maddie would like to carry on the business so a succession plan is in place to accomplish this goal. There is no simple way to divide the business into thirds and still leave the business intact for Maddie. Ben wonders how he can leave a financial legacy to the other two children.*

*After seeking professional advice, Ben decides to buy a life insurance policy to make up the difference. Ruby and Edward will receive their share of an inheritance in cash from the life insurance policy and Maddie will be able to inherit the business intact with no financial obligation to the other two siblings. Ben is able to accomplish his goals, treat all three children equitably and leave Maddie the business she helped build.*

Another benefit of life insurance is the ease with which it pays the death benefit. The death benefit goes exclusively to the beneficiaries listed on the policy. This shields the proceeds of the policy from fees and costs that can reduce an estate, including probate proceedings, attorneys' fees and claims made by creditors. The distribution of your life insurance policy is also unaffected by any delays in the distribution of the estate. Your beneficiaries will get the proceeds of the policy in a timely fashion, regardless of how long it takes for the rest of your estate to be settled.

Even though life insurance proceeds are generally free of income tax, if your estate becomes subject to estate taxes at your death, any life insurance proceeds would also be included in the taxable estate if you have any incidents of ownership in the policy. Having the life insurance owned by an irrevocable trust or owned by one of your children can keep the proceeds from being estate taxed. Under current tax law, neither Ben's small business nor the life insurance policy would be subject to estate tax. If Congress were to drastically change current estate tax law before Ben and his wife pass away, Maddie might have need to request a portion of the life insurance proceeds to settle Ben's estate. As for now, the tax-free lump sum can be utilized for Ruby and Edward's personal desires and goals.

## AVOIDING POTENTIAL SNAGS

It's very important to review the beneficiary designations of life insurance policies to make sure they concur with your wishes. For example, if your will instructs your assets to be divided equally between your two children but your life insurance lists only one child as beneficiary, the proceeds of the policy will only be distributed to the child listed as beneficiary. The beneficiary designation of your life insurance supersedes your will's instruction. This is important to understand when designating beneficiaries.

## CASE STUDY

*When Brenda turned 70 years old, she decided to investigate the benefits of life insurance. She wanted the security, reliability and tax-advantaged distribution that a policy would offer her heirs.*

*Brenda lives modestly on her social security benefit and a small pension, which meet her income needs. She has a Certificate of Deposit (CD) worth $200,000 that she has never used and doesn't anticipate ever needing since her income needs are already met.*

*After looking at several different investment options with a financial professional, Brenda chooses a single premium life insurance policy. She can purchase the policy with a $100,000 one-time payment and her beneficiaries are guaranteed a $170,000 death benefit **free of income tax.** The beneficiaries would receive $1.70 for every $1 that she deposits. Through a life insurance policy, Brenda instantly leverages her money by 70 percent. In addition, if she left the money in the CD, the interest would continue to be subject to income tax every year. Transferring half of the CD to the insurance policy will cut the annual taxable interest in half. This made a lot more sense to Brenda from a legacy standpoint than retaining all her money in the CD.*

Estate tax planning was a hotter topic a few years ago when the estate tax limits and exclusions were much smaller and the tax rates were higher than they are today. In 2008, estates valued at $2 million or more were taxed as high as 45 percent. Just two years later, the limit was raised to $5 million and the maximum tax was 35 percent. In 2014, the exempted amount is $5.34 million and the excess can be taxed as high as 40 percent. This reprieve from higher estate taxes will most likely not last considering the unprecedented size of the national debt. That debt has to be paid off at some point and taxing the rich to accomplish it has become the mantra of the current administration in Washington. Nevertheless, estate planning is still an important part of your legacy planning, even if you're not subject to estate taxes.

## CHAPTER 13 RECAP //

- Set aside time to plan not only your estate but your legacy. Doing so will increase the chance that your wishes, memories and assets will transfer according to your desires.
- Planning ahead can greatly reduce or eliminate the costly and time-consuming process of probate.
- Educating your beneficiaries on the advantages of a stretch IRA is a powerful way to leave a financial legacy.
- Make sure you understand the differences between *per stirpes* and *per capita* when making beneficiary designations.
- Life insurance is also a powerful legacy tool to provide the distribution of tax-free liquid assets to your beneficiaries.

# 14

# CHOOSING A FINANCIAL PROFESSIONAL

*"I do not trust easily. So when I tell you "I trust you," please
don't make me regret it."*

From the moment you dip your toe into the pool to the point you
start swimming laps, you're testing the water, getting used to it
and deciding if you want to proceed. This is not altogether different from choosing any professional to provide you with expertise
and direction. New relationships are usually tentative until we
gain the trust needed to feel completely comfortable with that
professional.

It's important to know what you're looking for in a professional
before taking the plunge. There are many who would love to
handle your money. Their enthusiasm does not necessarily mean
those professionals are qualified to handle **your** money according
to **your** standards and **your** goals. This presents quite a challenge
to those looking for quality advice.

The label "financial advisor" is often abused and misused. It can refer to a range of figures on a spectrum from credible (professionals such as CPAs, CFPs, and ChFCs or insurance professionals) to incredible (your uncle's next door neighbor who claims to have a lead on some undervalued stock about to be "discovered"). Many people claim to be financial advisors simply because there are no requirements in order to legally use the label. Asking questions and doing some research are the best way to determine the right advisor for your needs.

I have asked thousands of prospective clients over the years: "What are you looking for in a financial professional?" Some have no idea what they are looking for which is why they haven't found it yet. Others clearly know the answer. They tell me they are looking for someone they can trust, someone who is qualified and has their best interests at heart. This is clearly what I look for in any professional with whom I work - Can I trust them to do the right thing and keep my interests ahead of their own?

Choosing the right financial professional for your goals and objectives can be one of the most valuable decisions you will make for your financial future. Your professional will have influence and possibly even some control over your investment decisions, making their role in your life more than just passive. Your financial security and the quality of your retirement depends on the decisions, investment strategies and asset structuring that you and your professional create.

Finding such an individual or group is a trial-and-error task. Even when we're referred to a professional, whether it be a doctor or a plumber, it doesn't mean they are qualified to be **your** professional. It just means that the referee's experience has been good so far. It doesn't mean your experience will be good. You still have to trust enough to let that person in your door and into your finances. You still need to give them a chance to prove themselves, regardless of any pre-investigation you may have done.

## TWO KINDS OF FINANCIAL PROFESSIONALS

When it comes to financial professionals, there are two main types: those that take a professional approach to advising and those that take a sales approach. The type of professional you choose will determine the type of financial advice you'll receive.

**PROFESSIONAL APPROACH.** Financial professionals who charge fees for their advice are not unlike most other professionals such as doctors, lawyers or accountants. These professionals have been through a rigorous education program that usually includes a degree or designation as well as years of practical experience in their chosen field. They have been trained in many facets of the financial planning process and therefore **should** be able to provide objective, comprehensive advice to a client in the areas of retirement, taxation, insurance, securities and estate planning. Of course, a degree or designation does not by itself qualify that individual or company to plan your future, but it helps. It's important to remember that **half of all heart surgeons graduated in the bottom half of their class**. Obviously, there are other criteria involved in the choice of a surgeon or a financial advisor. Knowing that your advisor is well educated may add another layer of trust to the choice of him or her as your advisor.

The old adage "you get what you pay for" is an appropriate maxim to describe financial advisor relationships. Fee-charging financial advisors feel that their expertise, experience, education and ability allow them to provide objective, comprehensive advice. Such advice, in their view, is worthy of compensation. From their perspective, if you aren't willing to pay for good advice, you aren't a serious candidate for objective planning advice.

**SALES APPROACH.** Financial professionals who work on a commission/sales basis usually provide targeted, specialized advice. Brokerage houses, mutual fund companies, banks and insurance companies often provide financial advice on this basis. They have financial products for sale and the advice is targeted toward those products. If you buy, the advisor gets paid. If you don't buy, the advisor doesn't get paid. The main motivation for the advisor is to sell financial products. He or she may be very competent on the products available but receiving objective, comprehensive advice in areas outside of those products is not to be expected.

Since the organizations mentioned above specialize in securities (stocks, bonds, etc.), bank instruments or insurance products, the advice you receive is targeted toward those products. You should not expect an insurance-oriented advisor, for instance, to provide you comprehensive advice on the value of securities in your portfolio. That is not his or her expertise or training. The same goes for a broker at a brokerage house. Brokers specialize in securities. Although some insurance companies now offer securities and brokerage houses offer insurance products, the reason for this cross-selling is to retain in-house as much of a client's money as possible. It's to keep you from visiting the competition. The end result is still the selling of a financial product and the advice received will be targeted toward the products they sell.

Sales-oriented advisors may or may not have a degree or designation. Comprehensive education in areas that don't add to the selling of their respective financial products are not needed by those advisors. Some advisors do feel the need for higher education and are able to bring that benefit to the table with their clients. In the end, there is only so much time a sales-oriented advisor can spend advising a client before they have to move on to a new sale. Objectivity is in question when dealing with sales-oriented advisors.

Most independent financial professionals (those who do not work directly for an insurance company or brokerage house) also work on a sales-oriented basis. They usually specialize in either insurance products or securities.

A good way to explain the differences between the two types of advisors is with the following analogy. Assume you were having heart problems. You asked your primary care physician for two referrals to heart specialists. You visit the first heart specialist, some tests are run, and the specialist prescribes triple bypass surgery. Your additional questioning results in the same answer – you really need triple bypass surgery. And soon! Upon leaving you are told that there is no fee for the consultation. You are, however, asked to schedule your surgery. You want to think about it first so you leave without scheduling.

You decide to get a second opinion. You visit the other heart specialist. Similar tests are run and the prescription is three stents. No surgery is needed. You walk out of the office with a bill for the services provided. No pressure is applied to buy or schedule anything.

Whose advice do you feel more comfortable with? Whose advice are you mostly likely to follow?

The answers to these questions will help you determine the type of financial professional you should work with in planning the rest of your life.

## NARROWING THE FIELD

Once you've determined the approach the advisor uses to disseminate advice, it's also important to know how he or she is registered or licensed. There are three basic registrations that will further help you define the advisor's primary function.

**Insurance Agents** are licensed to sell insurance products such as annuities, life, disability, long term care and property/casualty insurance policies. Their expertise is limited to insurance products and insurance-oriented services such as income or estate planning.

**Registered Representatives**, better known as stockbrokers or bank/investment representatives, make their living by earning commissions on the sale of securities and variable insurance products. They are registered with a broker/dealer to sell products. Registered representatives are under no obligation to provide advice outside of the products and services they offer. In fact, for compliance reasons, broker/dealers often prohibit their representatives from giving advice outside the scope of those products.

**Investment Advisor Representatives (IAR)** are registered as representatives under a Registered Investment Advisor (RIA) firm. IARs have the ability to charge fees for financial planning. They also can charge fees to manage your money (Yellow Money). Often, they are licensed as insurance agents and/or registered representatives of a broker/dealer. This allows them to charge fees or sell financial products or both to suit the individual needs of the client. More importantly, **IARs are held to the highest standard of conduct in the financial industry – that of a fiduciary.** Fiduciaries must not put their own interests above that of the client at any time. Insurance agents and registered representatives are held to a lesser standard of conduct – the suitability standard. This standard only requires that a product be suitable for you before recommending the purchase it.

Investment advisor representatives are held to high ethical standards and are highly regarded in the financial industry. They often take a more comprehensive approach to asset management and financial planning. IARs usually operate on a professional basis, meaning they charge fees for advice. They focus on the big picture, not on certain financial products and services.

In choosing a financial professional, consider also the following criteria:

- *Credentials:* Look at their experience, the quality of their education, any associations to which they belong and certifications or designations they have earned. The two main financial planning designations are the Certified Financial Planner (CFP) and the Chartered Financial

Consultant (ChFC). Ask about continuing education programs in which the advisor is involved. Someone who has continued their professional education through ongoing training programs will be more up-to-date on current financial practices compared to someone who earned their credential 25 years ago and hasn't kept themselves current.

- *Practices:* Determine how the advisor is registered and how they are compensated for their services. Investigate the reports and analysis they offer to clients and any other value added services they offer.

- *Services:* If you are planning your retirement, you should work with someone who offers services that help you to that end. Asking an insurance agent, for example, about stock market strategies is seldom a wise choice. You wouldn't want to ask a stockbroker about the viability of indexed annuities, either.

- *Ethics:* Would you prefer an advisor who operates under a suitability standard or a fiduciary standard planning the rest of your life? It's your decision. Remember, you get what you pay for.

Once you've narrowed down the type of advisor you want to work with, the following suggestions will aid in your final choice of a professional.

**Ask for referrals.** One of the most common ways to find any professional to work with is through referrals. Asking friends, relatives, colleagues or other trusted individuals for a recommendation is helpful. A word of caution, however - **obtaining a referral to a professional should always cause you to do additional investigation.** A referral is just a name until you have thoroughly vetted it. It's not wise to assume that just because Jack has more money than you, using his advisor is the best decision. Jack may not need or want financial advice in areas in which his advisor is not qualified. Those areas of advice may be essential for you to address. In addition, Jack may like his current advisor because he's made a lot of money over the last seven years. But further investigation might reveal that everyone else made money, too, because the market was up.

The test of a true advisor is not how much money they can make you when the market is up. A monkey can make money in an up market. The best advisors are also the best at damage control. They are the best at minimizing losses, reducing your taxes and maximizing your income goals. There is a lot more to "advising" than showing impressive numbers on a performance report. It's also important to remember that nobody brags about their losses. Jack would probably not tell you how much money he lost in the first year or two of that advisor relationship.

**Ask for references?** Once you have selected two or three professionals that you want to consider, you may feel the need to ask for references. I would **not** advise this practice. Although many advisors would oblige your request, many will not. There are valid reasons for not wanting to offer references to prospective clients. None of those reasons involve the lack of pride in what the advisor has accomplished. I'll share with you my thoughts on the subject as a thirty-one year veteran of the business.

First, let me ask you two questions. Did you ask your current doctor, lawyer, accountant or plumber for referrals before you did business with them? Why, then, the financial advisor?

Second, every client I take on becomes a sacred trust. I would never reveal the details of any client relationship unless authorized to do so. Because of that trust, I do not feel it is appropriate to reveal to a stranger the names of anyone who has given me that sacred trust. If they choose to tell a friend or stranger on their own, I am grateful, but that's not my prerogative. I consider it a great blessing that many of my clients would readily agree, if asked, to serve as a referral source to strangers. I am not comfortable asking them if I can give out their phone numbers to strangers. To me, it's an awkward request.

Third, in the early years of my practice, I fell for this request many times and provided references. In the end, most of the people who asked for references seldom called them and seldom did business with my firm. It turned out to be a complete waste of time in most instances.

Fourth, if the advisor offers up a few names at your request, who do you think he's going to recommend, clients that have good track records with him or client's that don't? Then what good are the references?

My recommendation is to do your homework by following some of the other helps in this section to properly vet a potential professional relationship.

**Attend public seminars and workshops**. Many financial advisors offer free seminars and workshops at restaurants or libraries. This is a good forum to investigate a financial advisor. For an hour or two, you can sit and learn how the advisor works, thinks and communicates with no obligation to do business with them. Most seminars and workshops are sales-oriented, not professional-oriented, but that should not bother an informed attendee who understands the differences. If you like what you hear, following up with the advisor afterward can provide additional answers to your questions regarding that advisor.

**Use the Internet.** As a final step before picking up the phone and calling your candidates, do some digging to discover if anyone on your list has a history of unlawful or unethical practices, or has been disciplined for any of their professional behavior or decisions. Don't worry, you don't have to hire a private investigator.

You can easily find this information on the Financial Industry Regulatory Authority's (FINRA) online BrokerCheck tool: www.finra.org/Investors/ToolsCalculators/BrokerCheck/.

You should obviously explore the website of a potential professional and the website of the firm that they represent. The Internet allows you to go beyond the online business card of a professional to gain access to information that they don't control. It may all be good information! Or a brief search of the Internet could reveal a sketchy past. The best part is that the Internet allows you to find helpful information in an anonymous fashion.

Start with Google (www.google.com) and search the name of a potential professional and their firm. Keep your eyes trained on third-party sources such as articles, blog posts or news stories that mention the professional. You can also check a professional's compliance records online with the Financial Industry Regulatory Authority (FINRA) and the Securities and Exchange Commission (SEC). If you want to dig deeper, you can combine search terms like "scams," "lawsuits," "suspensions" and "fraud" with a professional's or firm's name to see what information arises. It's not likely that you'll find anything. Fraudulent financial advisors are no more common than fraudulent or inept doctors or lawyers. But if you do discover some negative information about the advisor, you'll be glad you checked.

## HOW TO INTERVIEW CANDIDATES

After vetting your candidates and narrowing down a list of professionals that you think might be a good fit for you, it's time to start interviewing. You can use the following questions during an initial interview to get an understanding of how each professional does business and whether they are a good fit for you:

**1. How do you get paid for your services?** This information should be available on their website. Find out if they charge an initial planning fee, if they charge a percentage for assets under their management and if they make money by selling specific financial products or services.

**2. What are your credentials, licenses and certifications?** Whatever their credentials or titles, you want to be sure that the professional you work with is an expert in the field relevant to your particular circumstances. If you want someone to manage your money, you will most likely look for an Investment Advisor. If you prefer a more comprehensive, objective approach to your planning and are willing to pay for the advice, some kind of credential or designation will be preferable. If they work for an independent firm, they could likely have a team of CPAs, CFPs and other financial experts upon whom they can rely for support.

**3. What are the financial services that you and your firm provide?** The question within the question here is, "Can you help me achieve my goals?" Some advisors can only provide you with investment advice; others offer insurance or tax advice. You will likely want to work with someone that provides a complete suite of financial planning services and products that touch on retirement planning, insurance options, legacy and estate structuring, and tax planning. Whatever services they provide, make sure they meet your needs and your anticipated needs.

**4. What kinds of clients do you work with the most?** A lot of financial professionals work within a niche: retirement planning, risk assessment, life insurance, money management, etc. Finding someone who works with other people that are in the same financial circumstances as you and who have similar goals can be an important way to make sure your needs are understood.

**5. How do you approach money management?** Professionals who are successful at retirement planning and full service financial planning will tell you that they listen to your goals, risk tolerance and comfort level and then pair you with an appropriate investment strategy. Working with someone that you trust is critical in this process.

**6. How do you remain in contact with your clients?** Does the advisor hold annual or quarterly reviews? How often do *you* want to meet with your professional? You may want to check in only once a year. You may want reviews more often depending on the services provided. Determine the right degree of involvement for both you and your financial professional. Determine how the advisor likes to communicate: in person, by phone or email.

**7. Are you my main contact or do you work with a team of advisors?** Some advisors prefer a more personal touch with their clients and will work directly with the client in planning situations and reviews. Others will meet with you once a year and have a partner or assistant check in with you every quarter to give you an update. Other firms take a team-based approach whereby clients have a main contact but their portfolio is handled by a team of professionals. One way isn't better than another but one way will be best for you.

## IT'S WORTH IT!

Finding, interviewing and selecting a financial professional can seem like a daunting task. And frankly, it will take work to narrow the field and find the one you want. But in the end, it will be worth it. Your retirement, lifestyle, assets and legacy are on the line. The choices you make today will have a lasting impact on your life and the lives of your loved ones.

Happy Retirement!

## CHAPTER 14 RECAP //

- There are two main types of financial professionals: those who take a professional or fee-based approach to planning, and those who take a sales/commission approach. Determine which approach is best for you.
- Financial professionals are registered as either insurance agents, registered representatives, investment advisor representatives (IAR)s or a combination of these registrations. How they are registered tells you how they do business.
- Don't be afraid to do your homework and ask the right questions when searching for an advisor. Finding the right fit for you can be worth all the effort.

# GLOSSARY

**ANNUAL RESET** *(ANNUAL RATCHET, CLIQUET)* – Crediting methods measuring index movement over a one year period. Positive interest is calculated and credited at the end of each contract year and cannot be lost if the index subsequently declines. Say that the index increased from 100 to 110 in one year and the indexed annuity had an 80 percent participation rate. The insurance company would take the 10 percent gross index gain for the year (110-100/100), apply the participation rate (10 percent index gain x 80 percent rate) and credit 8 percent interest to the annuity. But, what if in the following year the index declined back to 100? The individual would keep the 8 percent interest earned and simply receive zero interest for the down year. An annual reset structure preserves credited gains and treats negative index periods as years with zero growth.

**ANNUITANT** – The person, usually the annuity owner, whose life expectancy is used to calculate the income payment amount on the annuity.

**ANNUITY** – An annuity is a contract issued by an insurance company that often serves as a type of savings plan used by individuals looking for long term growth and protection of assets that will likely be needed within retirement.

**AVERAGING** – Index values may either be measured from a start point to an end point (point-to-point) or values between the start point and end point may be averaged to determine an ending value. Index values may be averaged over the days, weeks, months or quarters of the period.

**BENEFICIARY** – A beneficiary is the person designated to receive payments due upon the death of the annuity owner or the annuitant themselves.

**BONUS RATE** – A bonus rate is the "extra" or "additional" interest paid during the first year (the initial guarantee period), typically used as an added incentive to get consumers to select their annuity policy over another.

**CALL OPTION** *(ALSO SEE PUT OPTION)* – Gives the holder the right to buy an underlying security or index at a specified price on or before a given date.

**CAP** – The maximum interest rate that will be credited to the annuity for the year or period. The cap usually refers to the maximum interest credited after applying the participation rate or yield spread. If the index methodology showed a 20 percent increase, the participation rate was 60 percent and the maximum interest cap was 10 percent, the contract would credit 10 percent interest. A few annuities use a maximum gain cap instead of a maximum interest cap with the participation rate or yield spread applied to the lesser of the gain or the cap. If the index methodology showed a 20 percent increase, the participation rate was 60 percent and the maximum gain cap was 10 percent, the contract would credit 6 percent interest.

**COMPOUND INTEREST** – Interest is earned on both the original principal and on previously earned interest. It is more favorable than simple interest. Suppose that your original principal was $1 and your interest rate was 10 percent for five years. With simple interest, your value is ($1 + $0.10 interest each year) = $1.50. With compound interest, your value is ($1 x 1.10 x 1.10 x 1.10 x 1.10 x 1.10) = $1.61. The advantage of compound interest over simple interest becomes greater as each subsequent period passes.

**CREDITING METHOD** *(ALSO SEE METHODOLOGY)* – The formula(s) used to determine the excess interest that is credited above the minimum interest guarantee.

**DEATH BENEFITS** – The payment the annuity owner's estate or beneficiaries will receive if he or she dies before the annuity matures. On most annuities, this is equal to the current account value. Some annuities offer an enhanced value at death via an optional rider that has a monthly or annual fee associated with it.

**EXCESS INTEREST** – Interest credited to the annuity contract above the minimum guaranteed interest rate. In an indexed annuity the excess interest is determined by applying a stated crediting method to a specific index or indices.

**FIXED ANNUITY** – A contract issued by an insurance company guaranteeing a minimum interest rate with the crediting of excess interest determined by the performance of the insurer's general account. Index annuities are fixed annuities.

**FIXED DEFERRED ANNUITY** – With fixed annuities, an insurance company offers a guaranteed interest rate plus safety of your principal and earnings ((subject to the claims-paying ability of the insurance company). Your interest rate will be reset periodically, based on economic and other factors, but is guaranteed to never fall below a certain rate.

**FREE WITHDRAWALS** – Withdrawals that are free of surrender charges.

**INDEX** – The underlying external benchmark upon which the crediting of excess interest is based, also a measure of the prices of a group of securities.

**IRA** *(INDIVIDUAL RETIREMENT ACCOUNT)* – An IRA is a tax-advantaged personal savings plan that lets an individual set aside money for retirement. All or part of the participant's contributions may be tax deductible, depending on the type of IRA chosen and the participant's personal financial circumstances. Distributions from many employer-sponsored retirement plans may be eligible to be rolled into an IRA to continue tax-deferred growth until the funds are needed. An annuity can be used as an IRA; that is, IRA funds can be used to purchase an annuity.

**IRA ROLLOVER** – IRA rollover is the phrase used when an individual who has a balance in an employer-sponsored retirement plan transfers that balance into an IRA. Such an exchange, when properly handled, is a tax-advantaged transaction.

**LIQUIDITY** – The ease with which an asset is convertible to cash. An asset with high liquidity provides flexibility, in that the owner can easily convert it to cash at any time, but it also tends to decrease profitability.

**MARKET RISK** – The risk of the market value of an asset fluctuating up or down over time. In a fixed or fixed indexed annuity, the original principal and credited interest are not subject to market risk. Even if the index declines, the annuity owner would receive no less than their original principal back if they decided to cash in the policy at the end of the surrender period. Unlike a security, indexed annuities guarantee the original premium and the premium is backed by, and is as safe as, the insurance company that issued it (subject to the claims-paying ability of the insurance company).

**METHODOLOGY** *(ALSO SEE CREDITING METHOD)* – The way that interest crediting is calculated. On fixed indexed annuities, there are a variety of different methods used to determine how index movement becomes interest credited.

**MINIMUM GUARANTEED RETURN** *(MINIMUM INTEREST RATE)* – Fixed indexed annuities typically provide a minimum guaranteed return over the life of the contract. At the time that the owner chooses to terminate the contract, the cash surrender value is compared to a second value calculated using the minimum guaranteed return and the higher of the two values is paid to the annuity owner.

**OPTION** – A contract which conveys to its holder the right, but not the obligation, to buy or sell something at a specified price on or before a given date. After this given date the option ceases to exist. Insurers typically buy options to provide for the excess interest potential. Options may be American style whereby they may be exercised at any time prior to the given date, or they may have to be exercised only during a specified window. Options that may only be exercised during a specified period are European-style options.

**OPTION RISK** – Most insurers create the potential for excess interest in an indexed annuity by buying options. Say that you could buy a share of stock for $50. If you bought the stock and it rose to $60 you could sell it and net a $10 profit. But, if the stock price fell to $40 you'd have a $10 loss. Instead of buying the actual stock, we could buy an option that gave us the right to buy the stock for $50 at any time over the next year. The cost of the option is $2. If the stock price rose to $60 we would exercise our option, buy the stock at $50 and make $10 (less the $2 cost of the option). If the price of the stock fell to $40, $30 or $10, we wouldn't use the option and it would expire. The loss is limited to $2 – the cost of the option.

**PARTICIPATION RATE** – The percentage of positive index movement credited to the annuity. If the index methodology determined that the index increased 10 percent and the indexed annuity participated in 60 percent of the increase, it would be said that the contract has a 60 percent participation rate. Participation rates may also be expressed as asset fees or yield spreads.

**POINT-TO-POINT** – A crediting method measuring index movement from an absolute initial point to the absolute end point for a period. An index had a period starting value of 100 and a period ending value of 120. A point-to-point method would record a positive index movement of 20 [120-100] or a 20 percent positive movement [(120-100)/100]. Point-to-point usually refers to annual periods; however the phrase is also used instead of term end point to refer to multiple year periods.

**PREMIUM BONUS** – A premium bonus is additional money that is credited to the accumulation account of an annuity policy under certain conditions.

**PUT OPTION** *(ALSO SEE CALL OPTION)* – Gives the holder the right to sell an underlying security or index at a specified price on or before a given date.

**QUALIFIED ANNUITIES** *(QUALIFIED MONEY)* – Qualified annuities are annuities purchased for funding an IRA, 403(b) tax-deferred annuity or other type of retirement arrangements. An IRA or qualified retirement plan provides the tax deferral. An annuity contract should be used to fund an IRA or qualified retirement plan to benefit from an annuity's features other than tax deferral, including the safety features, lifetime income payout option and death benefit protection.

**REQUIRED MINIMUM DISTRIBUTION** *(RMD)* – The amount of money that Traditional, SEP and SIMPLE IRA owners and qualified plan participants must begin distributing from their retirement accounts by April 1 following the year they reach age 70.5. RMD amounts must then be distributed each subsequent year.

**RETURN FLOOR** – Another way of saying minimum guaranteed return.

**ROTH IRA** – Like other IRA accounts, the Roth IRA is simply a holding account that manages your stocks, bonds, annuities, mutual funds and CD's. However, future withdrawals (including earnings and interest) are typically tax-advantaged once the account has been open for five years and the account holder is age 59.5.

**RULE OF 72** – Tells you approximately how many years it takes a sum to double at a given rate. It's handy to be able to figure out, without using a calculator, that when you're earning a 6 percent return, for example, by dividing 6 percent into 72, you'll find that it takes 12 years for money to double. Conversely, if you know it took a sum twelve years to double you could divide 12 into 72 to determine the annual return (6 percent).

**SIMPLE INTEREST** *(ALSO SEE COMPOUND INTEREST)* – Interest is only earned on the original principal.

**SPLIT ANNUITY** – A split annuity is the term given to an effective strategy that utilizes two or more different annuity products – one designed to generate monthly income and the other to restore the original starting principal over a set period of time.

**STANDARD & POOR'S 500** *(S&P 500)* – The most widely used external index by fixed indexed annuities. Its objective is to be a benchmark to measure and report overall U.S. stock market performance. It includes a representative sample of 500 common stocks from companies trading on the New York Stock Exchange, American Stock Exchange, and NASDAQ National Market System. The index represents the price or market value of the underlying stocks and does not include the value of reinvested dividends of the underlying stocks.

**STOCK MARKET INDEX** – A report created from a type of statistical measurement that shows up or down changes in a specific financial market, usually expressed as points and as a percentage, in a number of related markets, or in an economy as a whole (i.e. S&P 500 or New York Stock Exchange).

**SURRENDER CHARGE** – A charge imposed for withdrawing funds or terminating an annuity contract prematurely. There is no industry standard for surrender charges, that is, each annuity product has its own unique surrender charge schedule. The charge is usually expressed as a percentage of the amount withdrawn pre-maturely from the contract. The percentage tends to decline over time, ultimately becoming zero.

**TRADITIONAL IRA** – See <u>IRA (Individual Retirement Account)</u>

**TERM END POINT** – Crediting methods measuring index movements over a greater timeframe than a year or two. The opposite of an annual reset method. Also referred to as a term point-to-point method. Say that the index value was at 100 on the first day of the period. If the calculated index value was at 150 at the end of the period the positive index movement would be 50 percent (150-100/100). The company would credit a percentage of this movement as excess interest. Index movement is calculated and interest credited at the end of the term and interim movements during the period are ignored.

**TERM HIGH POINT** *(HIGH WATER MARK)* – A type of term end point structure that uses the highest anniversary index level as the end point. Say that the index value was at 100 on the first day of the period, reached a value of 160 at the end of a contract year during the period, and ended the period at 150. A term high point method would use the 160 value – the highest contract anniversary point reached during the period, as the end point and the gross index gain would be 60 percent (160-100/100). The company would then apply a participation rate to the gain.

**TERM YIELD SPREAD** – A type of term end point structure which calculates the total index gain for a period, computes the annual compound rate of return deducts a yield spread from the annual rate of return and then recalculates the total index gain for the period based on the net annual rate. Say that an index increased from 100 to 200 by the end of a nine year period. This is the equivalent of an 8 percent compound annual interest rate. If the annuity had a 2 percent term yield spread this would be deducted from the annual interest rate (8 percent-2 percent) and the net rate would be credited to the contract (6 percent) for each of the nine years. Total index gain may also be computed by using the highest anniversary index level as the end point.

**VARIABLE ANNUITY** – A contract issued by an insurance company offering separate accounts invested in a wide variety of stocks and/or bonds. The investment risk is borne by the annuity owner. Variable annuities are considered securities and require appropriate securities registration.

**1035 EXCHANGE** – The 1035 exchange refers to the section of tax code that allows annuity owners the flexibility to exchange one annuity for another without incurring any immediate tax liabilities. This action is most often utilized when an annuity holder decides they want to upgrade an annuity to a more favorable one, but they do not want to activate unnecessary tax liabilities that would typically be encountered when surrendering an existing annuity contract.

**401(K) ROLLOVER** – See IRA Rollover

Made in the USA
Charleston, SC
27 November 2014